# About the authors

**Judi Fisher** has worked in the areas of education, community services and management for more than twenty years. In her first book, *A Place at the Table: Women at the Last* Supper, co-edited in 1993, she discusses a unique Australian visual-art project. Since 2000, when she moved with her partner Rex to north-eastern Victoria, Judi has been freelancing as a writer and an editor. She also facilitates a network of community-service agencies in the Goulburn–Murray region. In this, her third co-authored book, Judi promotes community performing arts based on a program she implemented while she was director of the Preston Creative Living Centre, a community centre located in Melbourne. She and her partner have an adult daughter, Jaom.

D1573145

**Beth Shelton** is a choreographer and psychologist, and is completing doctoral studies at Swinburne University, Melbourne. She began her professional life as a founding member of the dance company Danceworks, of which she was later co-artistic director. She spent fifteen years choreographing dance works in dance companies and communities throughout Australia. Beth has taught in many of Australia's tertiary dance courses. In her work, she combines her interests in dance, embodied experience, psychology and community. She lives in Melbourne with her partner Ian and two children, Brenna and Alex.

Spinifex Press Pty Ltd
504 Queensberry Street
North Melbourne, Victoria 3051
Australia
women@spinifexpress.com.au
http://www.spinifexpresspress.com.au

Edited by Deborah Doyle (Living Proof – Book Editing)
Designed and typeset by Modern Art Production
Photograph of Judi Fisher by Deborah Parkinson, Women's Health Goulburn North East; photograph of Beth Shelton by Robert Colvin; other photographs as credited on the photos
Made and printed in Australia by McPherson's Printing Group

National Library of Australia cataloguing-in-publication data:

Fisher, Judi, 1945– .
Face to face: making dance and theatre in community.

ISBN 1 876756 26 8.

Preston Creative Living Centre. 2. Community theatre – Victoria
– Reservoir. I. Shelton, Beth, 1958– . II. Title.

792.22099451

# FACE to FACE

## Making Dance and Theatre in Community

Judi Fisher and Beth Shelton

SPINIFEX

*To everyone who's journeyed with us at the PCLC,*
*and to community members everywhere who work for social harmony,*
*equity of opportunity and creative responses to life*

# Foreword

The other day, I heard a man with a rich, melodious voice talking about the importance of process. He was being interviewed on the radio station I'd just tuned into. He went on to talk about measuring success and failure. A successful journey for him, he said, is one in which relationships – within the team, with the people whose country he is travelling through, and with himself – have been good. I was sure he was talking about a subject close to my heart: community arts, and so I kept listening.

The interview concluded with the man with the golden voice saying, 'If you've succeeded in reaching the summit but haven't looked after the journey, that success is hollow.'

The interviewer then thanked world-renowned mountaineer Sir Christian Bonnington for coming into the studio. I was left suspended between the image of daring and courageous acts performed on impossibly jagged rock faces and the wonder of working with communities creating art in equally demanding and extraordinary circumstances.

*Face to Face* is all about this. It is a tribute to taking care of the journey, an inspiring and practical mapping of perilous and exhilarating territory: making dance and theatre in communities.

It is a book about relationships. How do you create and honour relationships as an artist travelling through other people's lands? Or as a community member or organisation, how do you begin relationship building that will bear artistic fruit and well-being for everyone involved? And for future generations? Within these pages are a range of answers as well as many more questions that challenge the reader to deeper contemplation of notions of community, artistic achievement, inclusion, the social values we nurture and who *we* are.

This book is also very practical. It includes details of three arts projects presented from the one small community centre. Each project is documented from conception to the final dot on the balance sheet. The successes and failings of each of these projects are articulated in a way that has rarely been attempted. In this way, the authors are offering footprints to follow for other people walking similar paths. Many voices – artists, organisers, participants, audience members – are heard adding their insights to the collective wisdom about the steps that lead to the summit of a performing-arts program. *Face to Face* is an important guide for other people presenting community performances.

For me, this book is about placing words as close as they can come to expressing the wonder of adventuring into realms of creativity beyond the beaten track. No book can express the depth and breadth, the challenge and fulfilment of what, every time, is a unique journey. Some books can be a loving and experienced guide, a hand to hold when the light fades and you're not sure where to step. This is one of those books.

Meme McDonald is the author of several award-winning books, including *Put Your Whole Self In*, *My Girragundji* and *The Binna Binna Man*. She's co-written five books with Aboriginal storyteller Boori Monty Pryor. Meme began her professional career as Artistic Director and co-founder of West Theatre Company. She spent sixteen years directing theatre in communities throughout Australia and overseas.

# Contents

# Preface

Underpinning the expression of culture through art, dance and stories are the cultural values that strengthen the spirit. – **Elder Pam Griffin, Mungabareena Aboriginal Corporation, Wodonga, Victoria**

In 1992, a small community agency in a northern Melbourne suburb decided to take a chance. The Preston Creative Living Centre threw open its doors and its beautiful, light-filled spaces for local artists and residents to gather and make community performances. Resources were marshalled to support artistic and community processes, and the centre became the venue for a series of vital and engaging performances. This book tells the PCLC's story. We, the co-writers, met there at the beginning of the first performance project: Beth as the key project artist and Judi as the centre's director.

We saw how the PCLC came alive with this work, how it filled with people and energy. We saw people who'd been living in close proximity, unknown to each other, come together and begin to understand each other as they created something new. Over the years, we saw many a dance danced, many a song sung, many an object crafted, and many a story told. Just as importantly, we saw careful listening and deep connections evolve between people despite the differences that separated them. We saw people forge new understandings in a complex and fragmented local region. And at the PCLC, community performance became an integral and regular part of each year's work.

> A crowded hall, a sense of excitement – this is no ordinary concert. Something's happening to those people out the front: they're engaged, involved, touching the depths. There's gladness; an awareness of discovery; the relief of expressing deep feelings; a wonderful youthfulness on those lined, eighty-year-old faces.
>
> Ancient fears and prejudices are swept away; fresh and surprising relationships emerge; people are standing taller . . . and they've done it themselves!
>
> And for those of us in the audience, we're more than spectators: we've been granted the rare privilege of participating in this emerging community, and we're touched and enlivened by the experience.
> – **Audience member Mac Nicoll**

In Australia, this work is part of a new wave of engagement with community-based art making. There's a sense of blessed 'unstoppability' to this wave. Increasingly, people in communities across Australia are celebrating and grieving their histories, and making new links and meanings through being involved in community-arts processes. At all three levels of government, in aid agencies, in community organisations and in business contexts, there's a fresh recognition of the importance of this work for our shared future.

Currently, in social debate, it's being recognised that healthy communities are built on more than economic premises: that our planning for the future must include providing for a vital and inclusive cultural life. For cultural adviser Jon Hawkes, a society's health depends:

. . . first and foremost on open, lively and influential cultural activity amongst the communities within it.[1]

In the broader contexts of globalisation, increasing social isolation and endemic depression, the social gains of community-art making – fostering social links, articulating shared values and increasing community well-being – are precious and timely gains indeed.

In this book, our aim is to help create partnerships between organisations, artists and communities for community-performance making. We don't intend it to be a theoretical discussion of community cultural development through the arts. It's the story of one organisation's experience in community-performance making – from the philosophy behind the work to the nuts and bolts of actually doing it. We especially address the book to you if you're:

- part of an organisation that might consider establishing a community-arts initiative
- an artist or arts student who'd like to work in communities
- a community member who wants to initiate an art-making project in your community
- interested in forms of community cultural development.

Our aim is to inspire you with art making in community as being a viable, exciting and fruitful form of community engagement and to give you some practical support with the development and realisation of a project. As we were fumbling towards finding a clear form and effective processes for making community performances at the PCLC, we looked for resources that were practically oriented whereby we could read about the experiences, insights, choices, strategies, successes and mistakes of other people involved in similar work. However, we found very little. So we came up with the idea of writing our own book and making our experience available as a resource for planning and discussion for future work in other contexts.

We offer our experience both non-prescriptively and humbly: we have a healthy regard for the specificity of each community and context, and we understand that community performance's potential goes far beyond any formula or model. 'Old hands' might find that the book is simply a reference point for reflecting on their own practice. For newcomers, we hope that the information in the book might make life easier and be a basis for discussions among the project's collaborative partners.

In 'Part One: Crafting Our Stories', we describe the context of the PCLC's work, the northern Melbourne region, the local people, the centre itself, and the centre's values. We provide a project 'blueprint': a broad summary of the processes involved in developing and realising our community-performance projects. We describe the form and aims of the Community Performance Making Program, and give a detailed account of the first three projects. Beth Shelton, the key artist for *Once Upon Your Birthday*, describes the project and discusses the possibilities of community-performance making; Bagryana Popov, the key artist for *Spinning, Weaving: Trees and Songs*, describes the project and focuses on how the community's involvement was deepened through storytelling; and Vanessa Case and Christos Linou, the key artists for *Best Foot Forward*, describe their project and outline how they took the arts into schools, factories and the wider community.

In 'Part Two: Taking Care of Business', we draw from our experience general points, questions and issues that we hope will be useful in other contexts. We use our 'blueprint' to structure discussion of factors through which successful artistic and community outcomes can be promoted, and point out some possible pitfalls. We discuss project management, financial management, funding and budgeting in some detail; discuss the PCLC's strategies; and provide specific information and referrals to other resources.

Co-authoring can be tricky, even for the most seasoned writer. We've struggled with how best to voice our shared and separate experiences. It was clear from the beginning that we'd each be contributing out of our own areas of expertise: Judi in management and Beth in artistic processes. However, there were also major areas of shared interest, for example in the philosophy of the work. Also, whereas Judi was there for each project, Beth was there for only one. Writing about each project has involved the recollections of everyone involved, especially the voices of the key project artists. By the time we'd played with and edited various sections, we'd found that if we attributed one of our voices to each section, readers would probably find the book difficult and potentially confusing.

So in most of the text, we've decided to retain our first person plural pronouns and to risk having some readers perceive us as having had a symbiotic relationship during the projects and in the writing of the book. However, we thought it would be clear who was writing if we switched to first person singular – 'I', 'me', 'my', 'mine' – when we were attributing the authorial voice to either of us or the key artist/s who worked on the project in question. In this case, we've included the person's name in the section heading. We hope that in choosing these options we've voiced our experience in the most reader-friendly way we could.

One thing we clearly share is a crusading zeal about the value of community performance; fortunately for the reader, we've managed to confine it to one or two sections of the book. Nevertheless, we hope we've infused the whole text with some sense of the richness, liberation, creativity, intimacy and momentum of the work in practice.

Much in the pace and ethos of contemporary life whittles away the opportunities people have for genuine contact with other people. It's been our experience that when communities make performance together, space is created for a deeper engagement with other people and with individuals' own values, understandings and creativity. This playful, purposeful human contact – face to face – is transformative: it can change individual lives and revitalise our social structures.

# Part One

Crafting our stories

# 1 The birthplace

(PHOTO: VERONICA RODENBURG)

**Figure 1.1** The entrance to the Preston Creative Living Centre. High Street Uniting Church, part of the original sponsoring body, is on the right.

In this chapter, we describe the context for a community–performance initiative: the regional community; the Preston Creative Living Centre (PCLC); and the centre's philosophy, physical space and chosen activities.

A metre-high red shoe. Twenty watercolour portraits of shoe-factory workers. A group of pregnant women dancing. A five-panel, hand-woven tapestry of the Tree of Life. An old man's story told with grace and gusto. An audience watching, transfixed.

Could creations such as these be part of solving intractable problems such as social isolation, political apathy, depression and violence? The Preston Creative Living Centre drew on insights, both ancient and contemporary, to answer 'yes' to this question: it entered into art-making processes as a constructive way of engaging the local community. This initiative has been met by a resounding and energetic 'yes' from hundreds of people and many artists from the City of Darebin – a complex, diverse and changing inner-urban area of Melbourne, Australia. In the Darebin municipality, community performance has become a regular part of the year, and members of the local community, local artists and the PCLC have formed a productive partnership.

In this book, we tell the story of that partnership and the performance projects created through it. We're telling the story in order to invite other communities, organisations, artists and community workers to consider what they might achieve by engaging in community performance and to provide a resource for their work – besides, a good-news story is worth telling!

3

We begin by describing the geographic, demographic and organisational context of our performance projects. What kind of place is the City of Darebin? Who lives there? What is the PCLC? Who is associated with it? In Darebin, what 'background' values and social conditions exist through which community performance was able to develop as a viable and fruitful form of community participation?

## What is the urban context?

The Melbourne municipality of Darebin is located along several key northern corridors of transportation. These geographic arteries flow from the inner suburbs and surge towards the metropolis's outlying growth areas. Preston, a large suburb in the municipality, is situated with Reservoir, its northern neighbour, along the corridor of High Street, and the PCLC is located on the boundary between the two suburbs.

The suburbs include both older residential streets and industrial-heartland areas that are being hit by shifting economics and employment levels. Change is evident physically in the municipality's shopfronts and conceptually in its public policies.

Darebin's residents bustle between markets, small shopping strips and large shopping malls. The shop signs are written in a variety of languages, and many cultural origins and tempting food choices are revealed in them. School students go chattering by, each burdened with a large school bag and heading for a bus or train.

Historically, Darebin has been home to many types of industry, including the footwear industry. Today, the municipality's employees mostly work in manufacturing or retail.

Four significant social factors at work in the municipality are ageing, unemployment, recent migration, and fracturing of families. In 1999, the municipal council declared its main priority to be community health and safety, especially with reference to intentional-harm issues: suicide among men, bullying at school, drug use, and domestic and family violence.

# Who are the community members?

In council and associated publications,[2] the municipality's population is described as follows.

- Darebin is one of Melbourne's largest and most populated local-government areas. It comprises approximately128,000 people and 55,000 houses.[3]
- It has a diverse population: more than a third of its residents were born overseas, and the largest groups are from Italy, Greece, the United Kingdom, Ireland, China, Macedonia, Vietnam or Lebanon.
- More than a thousand of its residents are of Aboriginal or Torres Strait Islander descent.
- As houses in the suburbs closer to the city become less affordable, more and more young families and professionals are moving into the municipality's solid-brick, 1920s California bungalows.
- Refugees and recently arrived migrants are 'starting over' by finding accommodation in the municipality.
- A quarter of the municipality's residents are older than fifty-five.
- The municipality's unemployment rate is about 13 per cent, which is almost twice Melbourne's average of 7 per cent.[4]
- Clusters of mentally ill people reside in the municipality in order to access its support and services.
- Many artists reside in the municipality.

# The PCLC: celebrating life

In 1992, the members of the Preston congregation of the Uniting Church in Australia found themselves in a predicament that many contemporary churches are faced with. They were a small and ageing group of people with a large suite of buildings located on an under-used property. The members of the church community realised they'd have to re-vision their relationship with the wider community.

The members of the Preston Uniting Church Parish decided to establish the Preston Creative Living Centre to engage with the local community's identified needs, and to work with the diverse and often disadvantaged Preston–Reservoir community.

Metaphor allows for transformation. It seems to me that to understand art or religion, we must understand the workings of metaphor. Both are about myth making, and myth lies in the imaginal world, which might be called spiritual–soul stuff . . .
The ordinary becomes extraordinary. In that moment of knowing is the quickening of spirit. I must not forget to remember that imaginal life-force we are all heirs to. We are all artists.
– Alan Browne, in *Art and the Work of the Soul*, Augustine Centre, Hawthorn, 1999

The PCLC was created both for providing community service and exploring the way people express their discoveries and life experiences through art, symbols and rituals. The PCLC was to offer a safe place where people could struggle with the ultimate questions of life.

Paul Sanders, who was the congregation's minister at the time the community decided to 'open the doors', writes:

> The bringing about of this dream has taken countless hours, by so many people. It has meant being courageous and bold in imagining what was possible within the context of the existing cultural norms and forms . . . A community cannot take this road without itself being deeply tested and challenged . . . May the Centre . . . be a place of healing, story sharing, celebration and discovery.

## What is the centre's focused work?

By conducting community research, the PCLC identified two key regional and local needs: human relationships and creativity–celebration. It focused on responding to the needs by developing specific programs based on them.

### Human relationships

The Family Violence Intervention Program comprises MEND – Men Encountering New Directions – courses in behaviour change, and a separate support and discussion service for women and children who are caught in family violence.[5]

**Figure 1.2** Andrew Compton, who co-ordinates and counsels in the Family Violence Intervention Program, at work. Andrew has been a PCLC staff member since July 1992, and was a participant in the 1996 production *Spinning, Weaving: Trees and Songs*.

**Figure 1.3** Local residents and PCLC supporters Elsie Gibbs and Jack Hollaway viewing an exhibition in the Art & Soul Gallery.

## Creativity and celebration

The Art & Soul Gallery is located in the heart of the PCLC. Each year, the centre provides new and emerging local artists of all ages with exposure and training by enabling them to exhibit in the gallery. The Community Performance Making Program is another part of this intentional response to creativity and celebration, based on the idea that performance making can be a constructive tool for community engagement.

Community members and local artists collaborate and engage with the PCLC and each other.[6]

# What values underlie the Community Performance Making Program?

The PCLC was founded on the understanding that spiritual well-being and social justice are of the utmost importance. Inspiration for contemporary action also came from Ancient Celtic Christianity. In the Celtic church, healing and creativity were integral to the church's functioning in the world. Artists were an inherent part of the church's life and work – both visual artists, as evidenced in the surviving *Book of Kells* manuscripts, and performing artists, such as storytellers. Historically, metaphor and making meaning have been a part of religion.

At the PCLC, we recognised that the making of meaning and identity was essential for each individual and, in a broader sense, for the local community's health and vitality. Giving form to life by using symbols and stories is redemptive: in giving our experience form, we give it meaning.

Several specific questions emerged during that time:

- How can we value and share our life travels and insights?
- Will tendencies towards violence be constructively influenced by an ambience of creativity and artistic dialogue?
- Can human value be returned to people who are economically marginalised and socially restricted, as a result of their engaging in storytelling?
- When people migrate, where do they find new spaces for their past stories?

In a contemporary setting, we found that these questions and values resonated with the ideas of community cultural development – 'CCD' – and with the practice of community arts. Social justice and equity are central values from both religious and cultural perspectives.

In community cultural development, emphasis is placed on having local ownership of projects and decisions, building communities' capacity to be self-reliant and honouring the social value of diversity. In one definition, CCD is characterised as being:

> ... an ongoing process in which a community creatively determines and expresses who it is, what it is and where it wants to go.[7]

When community-arts practice is at its best, practitioners put these principles into action by engaging in participatory arts processes.

## What is the shape of everyday activity at the PCLC?

The PCLC isn't a large agency. It's run by a few committed staff members, many of whom have a contractual arrangement to work part time. It conducts focused programs and has a limited annual budget. The centre's community aims are also achieved as a result of the goodwill of:

- compatible agencies, through renting and sharing of the premises
- other community programs, through hiring the space and using it for activities that complement the centre's aims.

Let's go on a walk through the PCLC . . .

When you enter, you're immediately struck by the place's warmth and colour – including the colourful artwork displayed on the walls – as well as welcome and respect. Pauline offers a 'cuppa' from the kitchen urn while Daryl waits to have his counselling appointment with Andrew.

In the Art & Soul Gallery, Kirrilee is busy mounting a new exhibition of local artwork. Through skylights, dormer windows and cafe doors, beams of light flood on to the old polished floorboards of the internal gallery and cafe area. The exhibition is entitled Dear Old Souls, because the artwork has been created by the LaTrobe Retirement Village's painting group.

A three-year-old runs through, clutching her doll. Charging ahead of her parent, she knows which route to take to the childcare room, which is provided for intellectually challenged parents who are doing the parenting course. Her mother pushes a pram up the ramp into the group room.

Some workshop participants chat in the sun of the garden quadrangle during a break in their activities. A few other participants inspect the Aboriginal mosaic art-piece, in which the site's two histories of indigenous and more recent presence are linked through two images of the journey: the *coolamon* and the canoe.[8]

Elva, the volunteer receptionist, is busy answering phone calls from people wanting to contact a Kildonan Families First worker or make an appointment for relationship counselling with a LifeWorks counsellor or a worker in the MEND family-violence program. Yvonne, the accountant, dashes to the photocopier to run off a few urgently needed forms.

Julie, this year's community artist for the Living Newspapers project, is in her office preparing for a late-afternoon theatre workshop for homeless young women. The workshop is to be held in the Stageroom. Julie will finish just in time for the arrival of the members of the Darebin Amateur Repertory Company, who are due to have an evening rehearsal.

The PCLC is an environment that 'contains it all' for many people: new refugees, my family-violence clients, workshop participants, staff, local artists, people who have a disability. It's a space to be welcome, a free space for some. It has a lovely image . . . and is an enlivened picture of the arts, with the interaction of the gallery and the community-arts program.
– Family Violence Intervention Program Co-ordinator Andrew Compton

This evening, the caretaker will work late in order to clean the premises for the Chinese senior citizens who gather at the centre on Saturdays. At other times, he might be here to prepare for the Alcoholics Anonymous members, who meet on Wednesdays, or the members of the MEND behaviour-change group, who meet two nights a week.

Within a broader community, the PCLC is an important place for people to contact each other and converse. On no two days do you hear the same stories or have the same routines as the staff members and local residents interact. Today, the centre is a physical space for community stories to be told, new images to emerge and budding hopes to be realised, amid celebration and creativity, the making of spiritual connections, and the blossoming of family and social relationships.

**Figure 1.4** After a *Best Foot Forward* performance: Mukles Minas, Christos Linou and Liz Landray watching the video, and debriefing.

# 2 The blueprint

**Figure 2.1** 'The stars are ours tonight': community members performing in *Once Upon Your Birthday.*

In this chapter, we trace the ideas, values and research that influenced how the Community Performance Making Program developed, describe the program's form, and provide a framework for the processes through which the form was brought to life.

A blueprint is a plan for work to be done. How helpful we would have found it to have a straightforward, clear blueprint as we fumbled towards finding a clear form and devising effective processes for making community performances at the Preston Creative Living Centre.

However, no document of this type existed – nor could it exist. In a way, in community arts, a blueprint is created every time an initiative is created, because the character of the blueprint is unique to the context of the performance making.

In order to work out the best shape for making community performances at the PCLC, we had to understand our region and to articulate and integrate ideas and values from three sources: the PCLC, artists, and community members – in other words, fumbling, investigating and integrating are crucial parts of the process. In this chapter, we write a bit about the thinking and research that lay behind the Community Performance Making Program, and describe the program's basic form and aims.

As we were writing, though, we realised that in telling you about the program's structural aspects, we weren't revealing very much about the practice of the projects – the processes involved and what it takes to make it all happen.

We therefore looked back over the experience of three very different performance projects at the PCLC. We decided to develop our own 'blueprint', which is essentially a diagram in which we broadly summarised the community and artistic processes that have proven to be integral to having successful outcomes. It's a 'broad brushstroke' view of a project's stages, through processes to outcomes.

Our blueprint isn't a project design; it's a broad summary of the areas of work involved in our projects as well as a tool for us to use in discussing our experience. We hope that in including it, we also provide a useful discussion tool for people who are conceptualising and planning their own projects.

## Seeing the possibilities

For us, a first step towards bringing to life the PCLC's commitment to community creativity was to investigate arts activity and artists in our region: what was the status quo?

In 1995, when we conducted our research, the results served to confirm what people in the area had long known: very few opportunities existed for Preston–Reservoir residents to have creative-arts experiences. According to our research, the situation hadn't arisen because the area lacked artists; in fact, quite a number of them lived in these suburbs.

Stephanie Francis, who at the time was the PCLC's Community Arts Co-ordinator, organised some meetings for local artists. The artists said that they felt isolated in Preston–Reservoir. They often had no point of contact with other artists or with members of their local community. They felt as if their art was separate from where they lived. For many of them, it was a struggle to survive financially.

Some of the artists expressed interest in forming an artists' network. Many were also interested in working in and for their community, but believed they needed some training and experience in order to do this work.

Stephanie and we two ended up having several manic, coffee-fuelled conversations in which we thought about how we could use the PCLC, with its beautiful – but at the time often empty – spaces, to contribute to drawing local artists and community members together. In front of us rose the possibility of a vibrant local-arts culture in which artists would be connected to each other and to the community; community members would explore artistic forms and make their own work; and there'd be a lively, home-grown artistic presence at local events, and in local environments and beyond.

It became clear to us that at the PCLC, we were well placed to make links and marshall resources. The organisation could become a point of contact between artists and community members, and we could use it to help resource activities and connections. This commitment found its form in an annual program we entitled the Community Performance Making Program.

## The form of the Community Performance Making Program

The idea behind the program is simple: each year, an experienced community artist from the region works at the PCLC and collaborates with community members to make a performance, and facilitates the process of helping other local artists to become skilled and confident in working with their community.

A community-performance initiative can take many forms: it can be a one-off or recurrent project or an ongoing program, and in it, 'community' can be defined as being a specific group or community of interest, or a regional approach can be taken. Artists can either be drawn from the community itself or come from another place.

At the PCLC, the annual and regional approach we took is well suited to the centre's aims and resources. The PCLC's model has both short- and long-term effects on local participation in art making. In each annual performance, there's a substantial impact

'Creative living' can mean so many things to different people. I'd brought with me an arts focus; for me, therefore, 'creative living' means dance, music, visual arts, singing – and creating opportunities for people to do these things, no matter what their age or background.
– PCLC Community Arts Co-ordinator (1996–97) Stephanie Francis

on the community in the short term. Also, because the program continues year after year, its presence becomes an established part of community life, and members of the community can be more proactive in accessing and directing it.

Because we make it a priority to employ and train local artists, the skills and networks developed through each project remain in the area, and a contribution is made to the area's ongoing creative culture. Although developing each project is clearly a big commitment for a small, multi-purpose organisation such as the PCLC, the program has proven to be manageable and viable over several years now.

*To have a balanced and creative society, it's vital and central that the artist have a place in the country's 'soul-space'. How do we encourage members of the existing generation to engender a soul-space of creativity: within families, cultural groups or belief systems? through local-council support, philanthropic efforts or governmental philosophy? Can we find a common commitment? How might we prepare a future that includes this common commitment? In many ways, the response has to be a 'whole of society' one. – Judi*

## The aims

The aims of the Community Performance Making Program emerged from the research, ideas and values we've described, and have been honed over five years by way of project evaluations. The aims remain the backbone of the work. We list them as follows.

1. To provide Preston–Reservoir residents with a high-quality arts experience
2. To create a supportive environment in which community members can participate in creating a performance, and in which the participants forge links with each other and during the process identify themselves as being members of the local community
3. To provide an opportunity for a local artist – an acknowledged artist in his or her field – to extend his or her own learning by participating in the artist-in-residence project

4. To transfer some of the skills to other local artists, by conducting workshops or in the process of developing the annual performance
5. To contribute to the PCLC's life by making people aware of our community's musical, theatrical, storytelling and artistic dimension and revealing the centre to be a resource for local residents and an arts space

## Our blueprint

We've reflected carefully on the work to date in order to identify the processes that to us seemed to be critical for a successful collaboration between community members, artists and the PCLC. In the diagram in Figure 2.2 on page 16, we provide a broad summary of the artistic and community processes involved in developing a project.

In chapters 3, 4 and 5, we refer to the blueprint as we tell the stories of the first three projects in the Community Performance Making Program:

* *Once Upon Your Birthday*
* *Spinning, Weaving: Trees and Songs*
* *Best Foot Forward*.

In Chapter 7, we continue fleshing out the blueprint by drawing on the three projects in order to discuss issues related to each of the five broad areas: origins, conception, processes, outcomes, and evaluation.

If you were especially interested in, say, how the ideas for a project might be generated, you could take note of each project's origins and conceptions as discussed in the project chapters; turn to Chapter 7 and read the discussion about this area; turn to Chapter 8 to check for any hidden difficulties in this area; and read Chapters 9 and 10 to find out about related management and funding.

In the blueprint, we use a linear form to summarise the processes involved in creating a project; however, nothing in this messy world is ever this tidy! Some steps along the way 'loop back' and influence things that have already been decided. For example, although the initial concept for the project is the stepping-off point for the creative process, the project concept will be altered and honed as a result of the creative process.

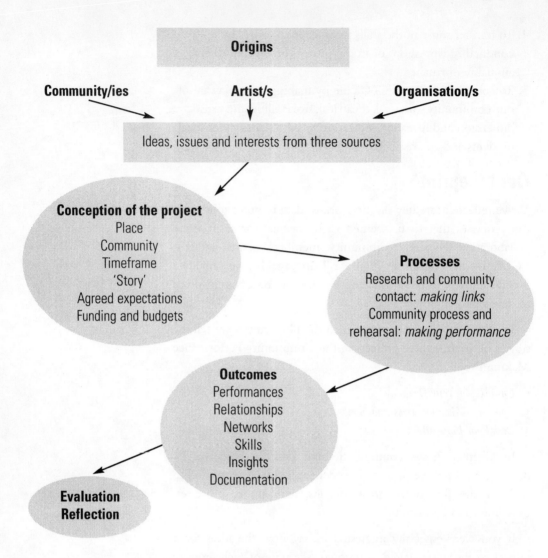

**Origins**

Community/ies     Artist/s     Organisation/s

Ideas, issues and interests from three sources

**Conception of the project**
Place
Community
Timeframe
'Story'
Agreed expectations
Funding and budgets

**Processes**
Research and community
contact: *making links*
Community process and
rehearsal: *making performance*

**Outcomes**
Performances
Relationships
Networks
Skills
Insights
Documentation

**Evaluation
Reflection**

Also, we've characterised the project's origins as coming from the interests of each of the three sources: the community, the artist and the host organisation (the PCLC), and as being brought together during the project's conception. Although we think it's very important that each group be represented when decisions are being made about the project, the collaborative partners can have varying relative weights of input at various stages of the project, and the original initiative can come from any one of the partners. Rather than be 'set in concrete' at the outset, the relationship between the artists, the host organisation and the community members is re-negotiated at each stage of the project.

**Figure 2.2** A process blueprint for the first three projects in the Community Performance Making Program.

Another point we must make is that not all performance projects are designed to go through this sequence once. For example, in our third project, *Best Foot Forward*, a series of workshops and performances was constructed in various contexts for various purposes.

## 'Both sides now': a reflection from Beth

*In late November 2000, I had the pleasure of simply sitting and watching a community-based performance. I was led to reflect on some of the rich layers of experience involved . . .*

*It's glowing dusk at the Return of the Kingfisher festival. I'm walking on a white-stone path lit by lanterns. I come upon something exquisite: fitted into the fork of a tree, a white-paper screen lit from behind by flame. On the screen, two delicate, filigreed shadow-birds dance. I watch them chase each other to the music of a harp, the soft splashing of the Merri Creek and birds calling the end of the day. The moment is delicate and pure: birds of theatre dancing in the fall of the day.*

*But when we move further down the path, our front-on view becomes a side view. Now we see the acts of creation that set the birds flying. Now we see young women working in tandem, one with her feet spread apart, knees bent, and balancing a large fire-stick on her body. She needs strength and resolve to hold the fire steady and light the screen. In front of her, two more women dance an agile duet, guiding the sticks of the bird puppets. Each partner's movements are attuned to the other's, to their birds and to the bush floor. Their whole bodies are alive with their task. A fourth woman sits, her feet firmly planted, playing the harp.*

*This view from the side isn't the transcendent, magical view of the front; it's dynamic and effortful. From this perspective, we see people working together to create an image of what's important to them in their place. From here, we see the commitment, the connections and the co-operation that underlie the creation of the performance image.*

When we were first thinking about the potential of community performance in Preston–Reservoir, both the 'front view' and the 'side view' were firmly in our minds. We wanted to support meaningful artistic and community processes from which long-term social benefits would flow for the area. And we knew that in community-performance making, these two sets of concerns are inseparable.

# 3 The beginnings

**Project 1:** *Once Upon Your Birthday*
**Key artist:** Beth Shelton

DESIGN: TINA BAGGIO

**Figure 3.1** A graphic used to promote the project.

In this chapter, we describe the PCLC's first performance project, *Once Upon Your Birthday*, which was based on the event of birth and the reception of infants into their community. We describe the performance itself and how the project developed, and provide an evaluation of the project's strengths and weaknesses.

## Developing a community-performance event about birth

I imagine the birth-song that resounds at every moment as women give birth: sweetness, power and pain, given full-bodied voice – 'singing the baby in'. The song is neverending; it shifts, settles, and shifts again, continually encircling the earth.
– **Birth educator and project performer Rhea Dempsey**

No one in the world knew what truth was till someone had told a story.

On the twenty-fourth of November 1996, about 350 people gathered at the Preston Creative Living Centre to perform in and witness *Once Upon Your Birthday*. For many months before the date, people had been gathering, telling and listening to stories; dancing; making stars and fire images; belting out drum rhythms; and sharing their experiences, thoughts and feelings about birth.

People came from many places. They were parents, midwives, older people, people bringing their own specific cultural perspectives, pregnant women, children, infants. Through the process, three understandings evolved, as follows.

- New ways of seeing birth
- A re-valuing of the birth event itself and of the powerful feelings that surround it
- A delight in the way the community is transformed when someone new arrives

Out of these understandings grew performance images in dance, song, drumming, storytelling and fire-image making,[9] which were threaded together to form a performance journey that was in turn funny, sad, surprising, down to earth, miraculous, finely honed and on the edge of chaos – something like the event of birth itself.

## Performance of *Once Upon Your Birthday*

Both spatially and thematically, the performance was structured into three areas:

1. anticipation
2. labour and birth
3. reception.

### Anticipation

A light-filled gallery area that featured dancers, singers and storytellers popping up in unexpected places was the 'waiting room': a place to evoke the anticipation of birth.

### Labour and birth

The audience progressed into a large theatre space, which glowed with light, for focused performance images of the birth event itself: funny, joyful and sad stories; dance; aerial performance; and song.

### Reception

At dusk, everyone moved outside for food, music and a performance in celebration of birth as a transformative community event. The performance ended with drumming, fire-sculptures, and spontaneous dance led by a group of Ghanaian people.

**Figure 3.2** Telling stories about birth, rocking the 'moon cradle', and singing and dancing with the Ghanaian performers.

PHOTOS: PONCH HAWKES

The overall form of the one-off performance was a careful layering of personal story with symbolic image across the languages of dance, music, visual image and theatre. One hundred and ten people performed, and twenty volunteers acted as marshalls and food co-ordinators. The performance sold out to an audience of 200, in which all age groups and many cultural groups were represented.

The audience members responded to the performance very directly, with much laughter, at times with tears, and ultimately with delight. The positive feedback both on the night and afterwards was overwhelming. People felt they'd been part of something both universal and unique.

Pregnant women made performance images that involved new ways of moving and being seen as pregnant women. They danced to Jane Bayly singing her song 'Jump'.

## Jump

*Am I brave enough to jump right in and get my feet wet?*
*Am I brave enough to jump right into the black hole?*
*Am I strong enough to dive right down and carry up the treasure?*
*Am I brave enough to jump?*
*Am I brave enough to jump?*

Parents told their stories about birth:

## Birth stories

Olga:   Well, it was first thing in the morning, and I was on my way down the stairs, and the landlord was right in my face, and I'm like, 'Get nicked: I'm having a baby.'

Louise: I had my second baby at home. My two-and-a-half-year-old daughter, she was sitting over there, and I was in the second stage of labour. I was pushing against the wall: 'NNNNUUUUUEEEEEEEEEEEEEEEEEEEE!' And my daughter calls out, 'Hey, Mum: do you want a chip?' 'Nooouueeeee: I donnnnnnn't want a chip!'

John:   I went into shock. I was shaking. I'd been so into staying with Jill during the labour, I didn't expect there to be a baby as well!

Jo:     I lost control of my face muscles. I didn't believe anything so ethereal, so exquisite, had anything to do with me.

Olga:   By the time I had him, there were about twenty people in my room. It wasn't how I wanted it to be, but I remember holding him in my arms and feeling his back. He felt so pure. And no one had ever held him before.

Carol:  I could tell from the looks on their faces that something was wrong. The midwife had tears in her eyes. I don't know how long it was before they handed her to me. But she was perfect, absolutely beautiful. No one knows what happened. She didn't take a breath. My baby died before she was even born.

**Figure 3.3** The performance of 'Jump'.

On a long, suspended rope called a web, aerialists Darielle Crawford and Ryan Taplin made a movement metaphor depicting the intensity, danger and out-of-control qualities of labour.

Mothers danced a rocking, turning and 'presenting' dance with their young babies.

The role of the body in pregnancy,
birth and early nurturing: a rich field.
The body in relationship;
The body as a site for transformation;
The body in powerful process;
One body becoming two.

Midwives made images and told stories. In her role as angel-midwife, Rhea told her story:

**Figure 3.4** The aerial performance.

## Rhea's story

*I'm going to tell you a birth story. It was a home birth in Elwood. It was happening on a really warm summer's evening, just like tonight. It was a Saturday night, quite close to Christmas. Anyway, it was on the top floor of a block of flats in Elwood. And because it was such a warm evening, we had the windows open. And being Elwood, there were a lot of people walking around the streets, and the sounds of the streets were coming up and through the windows, and we were hearing them where the birth was happening.*

*But of course, as the labour was getting stronger and the mother started walking up and down the passageway, she was starting to really moan and groan and sometimes to absolutely bellow with these contractions. As well as the sounds coming up from the streets through the window, the labour sounds were going through the windows and down into the streets.*

*So, what with the warmth of the evening and the sounds around, I don't think anyone could sleep. And of course, everybody in the flats around knew this woman: they'd been seeing her walking around with her gorgeous round tummy. Over the past few days, they'd kept asking her, 'When's the baby due? When's the baby due?' And now, they could hear that this baby was due pretty soon.*

My absolute highlight was the woman on the rope with the choir singing . . . She was hanging and spinning by her feet . . . that sense of disorientation; the furious energy; the way the light caught her now and then. It was really like the chaos of that last stage of birth. I was in tears on the night.
– Performer Kerry Kaskamides

So, while Mum's up, continuing with the labour, and the sound's filling the streets all around, gradually a bit of an impromptu party's starting to happen in the backyard of the block of flats. So the friends and neighbours had decided, I guess, that they couldn't sleep, so they might as well come and join the whole thing. So a bit of champagne was happening down in the backyard. And the mother was aware that this was happening, and she thought it was fantastic, because she knew that everybody had come to support her and to welcome the baby when the baby was born.

Meanwhile, upstairs, Mum's working really hard: up and down the passageway, round the dining-room table, bellowing and moaning as the contractions grew stronger and stronger, until eventually, as the labour came to the time close to the birth, the mother – as every mother all around the world, every moment – as the baby was being born, she released the birth yell, the strong yell, as she released the baby out into her partner's arms. And downstairs, you could hear this great cheer as everybody heard the baby. It was fantastic. Then, after a little while, after the Mum and the baby, the Dad and the little two-year-old brother – who was now the big brother – had spent a little bit of time with the baby, the father took the baby out on to the balcony and held the baby up and said, 'It's a girl!'

And a little while later, after the Mum and the baby and the father and the big brother were tucked up in the family bed, it was quieter. I guess that by that time, the people at the party were able to find their way home and tuck themselves up in bed as well.

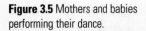

**Figure 3.5** Mothers and babies performing their dance.

PHOTO: PONCH HAWKES

# About the project, from key artist Beth

## Before we started: Where did the ideas spring from, and what were we aiming for?

Once, when I was very pregnant with my first child, I was standing on the edge of the water, looking out to sea and wondering about what giving birth would be like, when a huge wave came out of nowhere and literally knocked me off my feet. I found myself sprawled, breathless, flat on my back on the wet sand, not quite sure what'd hit me. In retrospect, this was a pretty good hint. When I actually got there, the intensity and enormity of the experience of labour did indeed knock me out.

After I'd picked myself up and found some rhythm in life with my daughter, I looked for representations of the experience of birth in visual art, literature and performance. I found very little, and most of it was stereotypic. I began to talk with other women and with midwives, and to record their stories. I realised that each birth story has its own metaphors, its own poetry, its own way of making sense.

Slowly, I started to see patterns among our individual experiences, and my desire to be involved in a community-based expression of the experience of birth grew strong.

I lived in Preston, and was part of the Uniting Church community that gave rise to the PCLC, so it was a natural step to look there for the project's home. Judi was keen to explore the potential of community-performance making, and saw the theme of birth as being a rich, inclusive starting point. In a collaborative process, with input from Judi and other PCLC staff, local artists and residents, the shape and priorities of the project began to emerge:

- We wanted to provide an accessible and quality arts experience in our region, which had a documented lack of this type of opportunity.
- We aimed to contribute to the development of a local community-arts practice by employing local artists.
- In 1996, the PCLC was a relative newcomer to its community, so we aimed to use the project to raise the centre's profile in the community, bring people into the

The event knit together on a simple level and on a profound level. The performers knew the purpose and truth of what they were saying. There were beautiful rhythms and spatial sense all the way through, and a clear sense of focus for the audience.
– Audience member
Shona Innes

The whole effect was celebratory and much needed in our community.
– An audience member

centre and let people know about the resources on offer there.
- We aimed to promote cultural diversity and cross-cultural networks.
- We wanted to make a lively, memorable performance event that'd be unique to its context and 'communicate' with its audience.

## July to September: How did we make links by getting the community involved?

### Listening

I went out and met people. I told them about the project, and I listened. I found that many people feel passionately about birth and hold birth stories that they want to share. I contacted maternal and child healthcare centres, playgroups, local midwives, birth educators and individuals. I heard something of what birth meant to different people in different stages of life and from different cultural backgrounds.

### Dancing

I offered local-community groups dance experiences. I gave one-off or ongoing workshops for groups, from toddlers and parents at playgroups to older adults at church-fellowship groups. As a result of these workshops, people sometimes came to project activities at the PCLC. Sometimes all the group members chose to be part of the performance, and I continued to work with them at their time and place, and invited them into the PCLC to have dress rehearsals with the rest of the cast.

It was these links, created through discussion and dancing, that made the project possible. They were the basis on which most people became involved, and they helped ground the eventual performance in the voices and experiences of people who had different relationships with birth and different stories to tell.

### Discovering the limits

Naturally, I sometimes encountered difference that I found challenging. One morning, all kitted out, eager and ready to go, with tape recorder and questions, I met with a lively older woman from a local Macedonian Church congregation. She told me some moving and poetic stories about her births, which had occurred long ago in Macedonia. However, she also made it clear to me that they were private stories that weren't to be shared, especially if men were present. She also told me that for her, dancing on church property was an act of sacrilege. She helped me see some of the project's boundaries.

## Discovering the potential

Members of the Ghanaian community, on the other hand, embraced and extended the project's concept. They recognised the performance's open-air section as being an 'outdooring' – a ceremony and party in which the new baby is presented to and celebrated by the village – and named it as such. This was a pivotal image in the performance.

# October and November: How did we make the performance?

During Week 10 of the project, we moved into performance-making mode. A team of artists joined the project, bringing a rich mixture of artistic forms. Performance-making workshops began on a regular basis.

At one inspiring workshop, some midwives described what their role involves during a birth. I recognised parallels with the role of a community artist. The midwives talked about recognising and trusting the process, being alert to problems, containing and yet challenging the people present, respecting, waiting, moving energy, touching, and suggesting change when it's needed.

In our creative process, the team of artists helped to 'birth' the various components of the performance: stories, drum music, choral song, fire and aerial images, and dance.

## Examples of the artists' contributions

- A group of parents developed stories about birth, facilitated by storyteller Julie Perrin.
- Members of local-church congregations, between the ages of ten and eighty, formed a community drum band, led by Clare de Bruin.

My friends were moved to tears and laughter by the performance. So was I. The whole performance was wonderful – creative; joyful; with poignant moments; and lots of enthusiastic energy from the audience members, who obviously loved it.
– A choir member

*Once Upon Your Birthday* was something you experienced rather than watched. It had everything – heart-wrenching true stories of birth and loss, side-splitting humour, breathtaking movement and song – and ended with fire, and throbbing drums, and more music under the stars. It took me to another place: to the lives of the women who shared their stories, and to my own stories of birth and pain, laughter and loss, and love.
– Journalist Clare Boyd-Macrae

**Figure 3.6** Painting some of the toddlers' faces in preparation for the performance.

- The community choir Petrunka rehearsed a score in which they wove together breath, vocal rhythms and Bulgarian folk song, directed by Bagryana Popov.
- A group of women made fire-performance images and fire-sculptures with Mahoney Kiely.
- Some pregnant women explored the association traditionally made between pregnancy and belly dance, and made their own new dance, helped by Marina Bistrin and Beth Shelton.
- Jane Bayly sang her own song for this movement sequence.
- For the final, outdoor part of the performance, some Ghanaian-community dancers and musicians organised a traditional blessing for babies.

Most of our groups worked separately, some at the PCLC and some in their own spaces. Although each participant understood the structure of the whole performance, when the entire cast came together for a dress rehearsal, everyone was amazed by the number and variety of people involved. Because the threads of the performance were drawn together at the end of the process, the production had to be meticulously organised in terms of production and stage management.

On the night, the event rolled out like a carpet. The performers were remarkably confident and purposeful. Lights, sound and cueing all went smoothly, and more than 100 performers came together to create a performance in which they told their stories and evoked their experiences of the mysterious and powerful wave on which infants are delivered into the world.

# An evaluation of the project

To evaluate the project in light of its five stated aims, we drew on the views of the arts workers, audience feedback, responses from the host organisation, and evaluation questionnaires filled in by approximately fifty of the project participants.

## Aim 1: To provide a context for a quality community creative process and performance in Darebin

### Strengths

- The birth event proved to be a powerful focus for community-arts work.
- The participants enjoyed and learned from the creative process, and several of them intended to pursue arts activities they'd discovered.
- People made new connections in their community.
- Parents valued the fact that the project was made available to 'northern-suburbs people' because arts opportunities are rare in the region.
- The audience feedback was overwhelmingly positive. The performance was satisfying and memorable for both the performers and the audience members.

**Figure 3.7** 'Out there': dancing during the performance.

**Weaknesses**

- Some participants would have enjoyed having a longer creative process.
- Some older audience members had trouble moving from space to space.
- Because the performance was for one night only, some potential audience members had to be turned away.

# Aim 2: To contribute to development of local-arts practice

## Strengths

The project was a vehicle for providing arts workers with on-the-job training. Of the project-team members, only two were experienced community-arts workers. Each team member took away a positive experience of having worked in the community and learned about some ways of working in this area.

# Aim 3: To increase community awareness of the PCLC as a local resource

## Strengths

- The PCLC's potential as both a community resource and an arts space was vividly demonstrated. One-third of the participants had previously been associated with the centre; the remainder were from various sectors of the local community, and most of them had been unaware that the centre existed.
- New links were forged between local groups and individuals.
- The publicity was targeted as broadly as possible in order to inform people of the centre's name and function, even if the project was not for some of them. As a result of these measures and 'word of mouth' about the event itself, the centre's profile in the community was raised.

**Figure 3.8** One of the graphics used on the promotional poster.

## Aim 4: To create an event through which cultural diversity is promoted and cross-cultural networks are created

### Strengths

- One cultural group, the Ghanaians, made a significant representation of their birth traditions.
- Individuals from many cultures participated, for example a Pontian–Greek dance group.
- The audience members perceived the event to be culturally diverse and therefore appropriate to its locality.

### Weaknesses

We'd hoped that the performance would include significant representations from a number of cultures, but this hope was realised in only a limited way. The contributing factors included:

- under-estimating the cultural sensitivity and complexity involved in speaking about birth with people from different cultures
- over-estimating the project's scope and resources.

## Aim 5: To re-frame and celebrate the body in birth

### Strengths

- People were startled and delighted to see pregnant women moving with such fluidity and confidence.
- For many people, the highlight of the performance was an aerial and choral metaphor for the most intense stage of labour.
- By including parents with their children and mothers with their babies in the performance, the physicality of nurturing could be explored, and some conventions of performance could be broken down in a joyous and unexpected way.

## The overall impact

The project touched a number of people – some profoundly. It had a substantial short-term effect on the local community, and will have long-term effects on community and arts development in Preston–Reservoir through the continued work of the PCLC.

Projects such as this make a different kind of performance possible. In *Once Upon Your Birthday*, new images of 'singing the baby in' were created that were unique to their context and deeply connected to their community.

**Figure 3.9** Another graphic used on the promotional poster.

DESIGN: TINA BAGGIO

## 'As we live': a reflection from Beth

For me, dancing with other people in a creative process is an opportunity to be in a different mode together. There's an unconditional quality, an 'utter-ness' in moving with other people, beyond explanation or rationalisation. There's space to connect to yourself and to other people differently, to risk new ways of being and, by extension, to create a different social fabric.

As we live, we inevitably create meaning; we're meaning-making creatures. In telling our stories and dancing our dances, we're able to share some of the meanings we've wrought, often out of pain and suffering, and to make the meanings a community resource. In this way, we refuse to live by competitive, 'winner takes all' social ethics through which a kind of lonely despair is created and individual lives seem unimportant.

It seems to me that now, in the early 2000s, we're deeply challenged to balance global and local perspectives, and economic and social values. These are challenges we all share, across communities, politics, business, human services and the arts. If we want to live in a social milieu in which we value responsible action, community connections and justice rather than apathy, alienation and disenfranchisement, we have to actively build this type of milieu: a place that's full of organic and unpredictable connections and rich with diversity. We live in the communities that we build.

**Figure 3.10** Beth and son Alex at *Once Upon Your Birthday*.

PHOTO: JUDI FISHER

# **4** The deepening

**Project 2:** *Spinning, Weaving: Trees and Songs*
**Key artist:** Bagryana Popov

DESIGN: ILKA WHITE

**Figure 4.1** The logo used to promote the performance.

In this chapter, in collaboration with key artist Bagryana Popov, we describe the PCLC's second project, *Spinning, Weaving: Trees and Songs*, which was built around family trees and stories. Bagryana gives a detailed account of the project's creative process, and provides an evaluation of the project's strengths and difficulties.

## Developing a community-performance event about family trees and stories

The forest neither spun nor wove;
All winter it lay still,
And when summer came,
The forest got itself up
And decked itself out
All in a green velvet,
All in green velvet.
– A Bulgarian folk song

*Spinning, Weaving: Trees and Songs* was performed at the PCLC on the twenty-ninth and thirtieth of November 1997 to a combined audience of 200 people. The performance was a piece of theatre of interwoven personal stories, some very funny and others deeply moving and profoundly sad. The stories, about key relationships and key moments in the performers' family trees, had been written during workshops by the performers themselves.

The staging was simple. Ten spinning wheels whirred on stage as the performers told their stories. All the spinning wheels were angled towards a superbly colourful woven-wool backdrop on which the Tree of Life was depicted.[10]

PHOTO: JUDI FISHER

The action of spinning linked with the metaphorical resonance of the stories: history being passed on, the flow of time and the cycles of life. Darebin residents, as storytellers, explored themes of meetings, change, separation, distance and nostalgia, and tradition and migration.

**Figure 4.2** The Tree of Life backdrop and some of the spinning wheels during the set-up stage.

Songs to evoke the time and spirit of the stories were sung by the cast. Singing the songs was a way to link memories and change scenes. The songs varied from traditional Bulgarian folk songs and Javanese lullabies to Anglo-Australian favourites such as 'The Road to Gundagai' and 'It's a Long Way to Tipperary'. The Melbourne Women's Bulgarian Choir, Petrunka, musically backed the production.

The members of the final performing group were between eleven and eighty years of age. They included retirees; migrants; both settled and recently arrived; parish members; University of the Third Age (U3A) students; young mothers; and single women: a cross-section of people, each of whom shared a rich reflection on his or her life and family links.

The stories were of a personal nature, and the audience members responded very openly. A depth of feeling was evident on both sides of the stage. A sense of relationship was central in both the project's process and the culminating performance. The performers forged strong personal links with each other. These links across community groups cut through the anonymity and stereotypes of a large urban community. It was powerful and moving to experience theatre in which the performers created a very human context for expression and communication on a deep level.

## About the project, from Bagryana
### How the project originated and was conceived

I'd heard about Catherine Simmonds's work with the Brunswick Women's Theatre, and I'd just come back from overseas and was looking to create a new project. I wanted to work with community members. There was a sense, for me, of the potential beauty of people's stories and the satisfaction of creating work through collaborating with community. I had the urge to try it.

Through a series of contacts, I found the PCLC. In my first meeting with Judi, she handed me a little booklet written by women who'd experienced domestic violence. There was a statement in one story: 'If I'd been raised that I had value, maybe I would have got out of it sooner.' That got me thinking about what we're taught, what we carry from the generations before us: stories both conscious and unconscious.

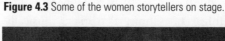

**Figure 4.3** Some of the women storytellers on stage.

PHOTO: KYLA JANE HUNT

## Pre-recruitment: the arts team

I had a very strong image of spinning wheels for the piece, so spinner, weaver and designer Ilka White was an obvious choice for the arts team. I then met Alice Nash, who was also experienced with community work, more on the organisational side. The three of us hit it off, so there was our arts team!

All the elements were there: the PCLC, Judi's support, the space, an office and a phone . . . But where to start? Between the idea and the reality is a hard road paved with a great many phone calls, many people and much work.

The members of the production group for the preceding production, *Once Upon Your Birthday*, had disbanded on the night of their performance. Although there was a tradition and energy in the space at the PCLC, we had no people to work with yet. The phone became the centre of it.

The beginning of the process was the dreaming. Ilka, Alice and I would meet in the mornings and dream up what we hoped the project would be. We began with some images: the spinning wheels, the poem 'The forest neither spun nor wove', some songs, and the need to hear and tell stories.

During this conceptual stage – twenty-four days spread over twelve weeks – several questions became central, and the participants later addressed them during the writing and generating workshops.

- What do we remember of generations before us?
- What events do we recollect and carry with us that shape our sense of ourselves and our personal narrative?
- What are the decisive turning points and moments in people's lives that shift things?
- What do we pass down to the next generation?

We were keen to create a broad, non-judgemental framework through which various stories would emerge: momentous or mundane, light or profound – whichever stories people wanted or needed to tell. As a team, we were interested in the detail and depth of people's stories and the stories from the generation before them, across differences of ethnic background, age and gender. Broader themes, such as migration, were also approached through individual experiences.

It would be good to show it elsewhere. I loved having older people to mix with and learn from.
– Performer and Petrunka member Geraldine Bate

## Sharon's story: 'Weaving My History'

*Alone.*
*I was the first one to be born in Australia.*
*The first of my family. On both sides:*
*On my mother's, and my father's.*
*No one had set foot in Australia before.*
*Alone.*
*No grandparents: no mother's parents, no father's parents,*
*No aunts, no uncles, no cousins, no second cousins, no in-laws,*
*No connections, no passing on. no hand-me-downs, no roots.*
*No warp, no weaving.*
*I feel unwoven.*
*Where do I come from?*
*Nowhere.*
*No – wait . . .*
*I wonder and wander.*
*I travel to find my past.*
*Germany: war, fires, bombing – but there I find my blue eyes.*
*Hungary: poverty, hunger – but there I finally find my dark hair.*
*France: change and occupation – but there I find my interest in art.*
*Poland, Russia: death and dislocation –there I find my ability to*
  *make the best of very little.*
*(I find my freckles in Scotland.)*
*Links! I have found small links!*
*I take them with me when I go back to my home.*
*The home I make myself.*
*I must start my own weaving.*
*I build my own loom.*
*A strung base on which I can weave new colours.*
*Fresh colours – free from the wars, the guilt, the blame.*
*I use the tiny pieces I have searched for and salvaged,*
*And fill the spaces with bright strings of colour,*
*Given to me by my universal family,*
*In place of my own,*
*So that I can weave a new cloth*
*To wrap myself and future generations in.*

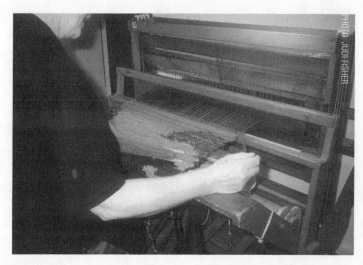

## Inviting people to become involved

We had to get people on board, and that's when the telephoning came in. We just rang and talked, and talked, and talked, in order to invite people, to explain the idea and to follow up links.

Who did we phone? A plethora of government and community organisations: the Adult Migrant Education Service (AMES), the University of the Third Age (U3A), the Thornbury–Preston Craft Workshop, the local neighbourhood house. We stressed that the art form was manageable for newcomers. We also phoned anyone I knew – people in shops, carers at my kids' childcare centre.

At the same time, Ilka was starting to involve people who were interested in the spinning and weaving. Over many weeks at the PCLC, a group of local participants first spun the wool and dyed the yarn, then, using five large looms, translated a Tree of Life design into a vibrant and colourful backdrop for the performances.

So we had both spinning–weaving workshops and storytelling workshops. With these both happening at once, we were still searching for the form. Each decision felt like a step into new territory towards shaping the ideas into a palpable form.

We advertised workshops, some in the day and some in the evenings. Alice and I were very nervous at the beginning: *Would anyone come?* For the first workshop, three women came along.

**Figure 4.4** A community participant weaving one of the backdrop's five panels.

Two of them, Greek sisters, told beautiful stories. It was a gentle beginning. Gradually, over the three months, more and more people joined the workshops. We collected all their stories, and typed up each story as we went along. The themes were 'grandfather', 'grandmother', 'parents', 'meetings', 'partings', 'births', 'marriages' and 'deaths'. By the time the three months had gone by, we had a lot of material.

The net was spreading widely. The twenty-five performers turned out to be a very diverse group: members of the local-church community; members of the women's choir; U3A students; Harold Osborne, who came along because he could fix spinning wheels; Andrew Compton, who was a member of the PCLC's counselling team; and Mukles Minas, who came from the Adult Migrant Education Service. Mukles came to every rehearsal, and learned enough English to be able to tell the story of his Iraqi grandfather's marriage:

### Mukles's story

*My grandfather, when he got married, was very old: he was fifty-five years old. When he was working in his workplace – weaving on the loom, making rugs – he worked with the same girl for many years. The girl loved him, but she was too shy to tell him. My grandfather didn't care about this girl – he was always busy with his job.*

*The girl's father was his friend for a long time. He asked his friend [my grandfather], 'Why don't you get married?' and encouraged his friend to marry his daughter.*

*My grandfather said to him, 'Are you crazy? I am fifty-five years old; she is twenty-five years old.' He said, 'Ask if she loves me; I'll marry her.'*

*Her father asked his daughter, and she said, 'Yes: he is a good man; he is honest, never doing bad things. Yes: I love him.'*

*And they got married, and had five daughters and two sons. They had many happy days together.*

Ria's story about her father was also part of the performance script:

PHOTO: KYLA JANE HUNT

## *Ria's story*

*My father sat on the doorstep on the weekends, polishing his shoes and listening to the radio and wearing a sarong, in Clayton South. He would do all his gardening chores still wearing his sarong, putting all the rubbish in the incinerator and washing the car, singing Javanese songs and his favourite Doris Day song.*

*When he was caught in the political upheaval in Indonesia, he and my mother decided not to risk getting put in prison, and left for Melbourne. He got a job translating, because he spoke English well.*

**Figure 4.5** Mukles telling his grandfather's story, and Ilka White playing the young bride.

# Workshop technique: the storytelling

Once we went into the workshop space, it was a very personal and private space.

People loved to communicate with each other, and did so with quite amazing generosity. It was a healing and gentle process, to have the space to tell stories about people important to us, about events that have passed and have never been articulated.

So there was an opportunity there in that beautiful sunny room to communicate on a level that you usually can have with only your closest family members and friends. And we gave each other unequivocal attention, the space to remember, and a depth of listening that transforms everything. The steps of our workshop processes were as follows.

- There was usually a physical group warm-up to relax and bring participants together.
- Then there was a meditative space: the group members would take their own place and enter into this space. They might sit or lie down and close their eyes, and I would ask them to remember something with a theme. Usually I would structure it with a specific set of questions to lead through things, for example meetings, a moment in childhood, a place. I would ask them to focus on all the important physical detail. I would ask about the sequence: 'And what happened afterwards? What did you love about the person? What did they give you? What did you come away with? What was most difficult about the person?' The balance between difficult and positive aspects of memories was important.
- At the writing stage, the storytellers would write it all down.
- Finally, we would share, reading our stories all in a circle, each having a turn, if they wanted to read. Sometimes, discussions would come up as other people would remember details or similar events.
- Later, as we approached the rehearsal time, people found simple and evocative movements for the telling of the story.
- We found songs that were appropriate to the stories.

The storytelling proved to be a redemptive exercise. If things came up that were really difficult, or heavy, or sad – in the exercise, or in the story, or in the performance – we would still come out the other end. The process of telling the story, of finding a contained and poetic form for experience, was both meaningful and pleasurable.

It was important to find the balance, in stories, between the difficult and the redemptive. Stories are never just one thing: they're complex and multi-layered. Even during times of tragedy and grief and parting, there is humour; there is the movement forward towards survival. In hearing and telling those stories, we recognise each other as being fully, utterly human. Following are two of these stories from the performance script.

## Cliff's story

Our lives mingle so many things together, I wouldn't know where to start. There are lots of things you don't know the answers to, and when you get old, you realise that you've missed your opportunity, somewhere along the way, to ask the right questions at the right time.

When I was ten – or about seven or eight – I was talking to my grandma, and she told me she was my grandfather's second wife. 'What happened?' I said. She said he was married, and his first wife died at childbirth with their first baby. And that sort of thing happened all the time in those days: women died in childbirth.

And then my grandmother had four children, and three of them died. The first was killed in the Great War. The second, a daughter, at seventeen, died of the flu epidemic; she was named Mary, after the first wife. The youngest died of TB at age twenty-eight. Only my mother survived, which is why I'm here today.

Well, anyway, that's my story, and I'm sticking to it.

**Figure 4.6** Community participant Norm Davis telling a childhood story about his family's Saturday-evening bath routine.

## Judith's story

They lived and married in a small country town, the daughter of a pioneer farmer and the son of a city-bound labourer.

My sister was born in the summer of 1937. Hot with the threat of bushfires – a typical Australian summer.

It was just before Australia Day. The men of the district, on foot and carrying water-filled knapsacks, were fighting scattered fires, while their wives, mothers and sisters sustained them with tea and sandwiches. My mother, a pioneer's daughter, was pregnant with her first child.

Her pioneer father, who owned one of the few cars in the district, drove her to the bush nursing hospital, twenty long miles away, leaving her in the care of the midwives.

In the early hours of Australia Day, the twenty-sixth of January, a fire broke out in the centre of the small community, burning the post office, the grocery store, and – oh, most terribly, most awfully – burning the pub. The townspeople were devastated.

*The fire was eventually beaten, and word came through that as the town was burning, the pioneer's daughter had given birth to a baby girl, a tiny, red-faced bundle – with flaming-red hair: a true Australia Day baby.*

## Structuring the theatre piece

From the pool of workshop material, stories were chosen and ordered into an overall shape. I wove them together according to themes and the rhythm of the piece, without changing the writing.

The script itself was finalised four weeks before performance. We rehearsed on a one-to-one basis [that is, Bagryana with the participant-performer]. There were four intensive weekend rehearsals to bring the whole ensemble together.

What is important is to find the style of the piece in such a way that the performers will be supported to the maximum. It is about finding a way to help people be visible and to be heard in such a way that they are comfortable, and to allow their story to come through. People need to claim their performance and be proud of it. Simplicity and cleanness of staging actually take an enormous amount of rehearsal.

During the final stage, I had to demand a firm commitment from all the performers. The ensemble is very important, and the commitment to coming together on time is crucial to the project's life.

## An evaluation of the project

At the end of the project, thirteen of the performers completed an evaluation form. The themes that recur in their remarks are:

- great satisfaction in making links with other people from the community, especially the older people
- important personal journeys made, both emotional and healing
- discovering the value of stories and family histories
- pleasure in performing
- sense of fulfilment, achievement and recognition from the audience

- desire to have had more time to rehearse, especially individually
- desire for more audiences to see the show
- enjoyment of the mix of people and styles of performance
- gratitude for the opportunity to have been involved.

In an internal evaluation conducted among managers and artists, the main focus was on strengths and difficulties faced during the project.

## Strengths

1. The members of the following four identifiable groups benefited from being involved in the project.
   a) Community members, through being involved in a quality arts project through which their personal stories were given a voice and affirmed
   b) The audience members, by being offered a moving experience through which their individual emotional journeys were affirmed
   c) All the artists, through having their skills and experience of theatre practice extended, and through having their understanding of the demands and possibilities of community arts established
   d) PCLC programs, through raising people's awareness of the centre as an arts space and a community resource
2. A year after the performance, in September 1998, the project was re-mounted at a professional-theatre venue.
3. The woven backdrop was featured in two other productions: as an invited exhibition and as part of a stage design.[11]

## Difficulties

1. It was time consuming recruiting the participants. Few people were attracted as a result of the printed publicity. The people who entered into the process did so on trust. The arts-team members spoke in person to each of the final twenty-five performers.

2. The arts-team members gave priority to having men as well as women involved, because in our experience, it's much more common for women to be part of arts projects. The final ensemble of twenty-five included six males.

I was curious and glad to be involved in a community project. At the end, I thought the performance was extremely successful, not only from an audience perspective but on behalf of the performers, who all made personal journeys of their own.
– Performer Edwina Harrison

3. Another priority was to involve residents from a non-English speaking background in order to represent the Darebin community's cultural diversity. Because there was a cultural and language divide, it was difficult to communicate the nature of the project, especially to the newly arrived residents, who often have very different concerns, most notably finding and maintaining employment, reuniting with absent family members, and finding housing.

4. As the end-performance dates approached, it was difficult to gather everyone to come to the rehearsals. It was definitely a challenge to maintain the delicate balance involved in urging people to be constant and alienating them. Likewise, the rehearsal style had to be varied in intensity according to the individual's skills and needs. Also, it was difficult to form a confident picture of the whole, because we were working individually with people or in separate groups until the very end.

## The project's overall impact

Both the participants and the audience members were enriched by the performance's impact and beauty. A number of people's lives were touched as a result of the friendships and ongoing artistic connections that were forged.

The quality of the work itself contributed to the PCLC's growing reputation in community arts, and as a result, the number of local residents and artists interested in the PCLC's creative work increased.

And the impact on me?

## 'Profound change': a reflection from Bagryana

As the director, I found the project a rich personal and artistic experience. It was deeply moving because it brought together such disparate individuals and groups into a supportive ensemble with an atmosphere of warmth, humour and sensitivity to one another's stories. There was a genuine sense of community, of people coming together and being very open and involved with one another.

I changed profoundly – not just as an artist but as a person. I feel so much fuller and more three dimensional. I couldn't – wouldn't – want to let it go now. There's something about working with community that engages a kind of 'ego-lessness' in me because it is so much about them and doing everything to bring them forward – all your energy and ego go into that. It's almost similar to parenting. You're working towards another person's working or flourishing, and that's the focus; that's where the energy lies. This work really filled out my understanding and sense of myself, and the possibility of theatre. But it also offered that ability of communicating so deeply and so finely.

I have since gone on to direct three community-arts projects: two based in Darebin and one at the Melbourne Museum Complex, in Carlton. The PCLC project was formative to my path as an artist working with community. It gave me my first important step in that direction.

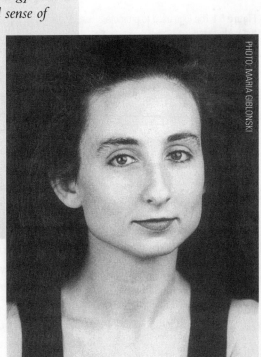

Figure 4.7 Bagryana.

# Into new territory

**Project 3:** *Best Foot Forward*
**Key artists:** Vanessa Case and Christos Linou
In partnership with the Diana Ferrari Shoe Factory

DESIGN: CATRINE BERLATIER

**Figure 5.1** The logo used to promote the performance.

In this chapter, in collaboration with key artists Vanessa and Christos, we describe the PCLC's third project, *Best Foot Forward*, which was based on images of shoes, feet and dance. The project was one of the first artistic links forged between performing artists and industry workers in Darebin, through formation of a partnership with workers at a local shoe factory. During the project, the artists also worked with people who had a disability as well as with children from local schools. We describe the project's creative process in some detail, and provide an evaluation of the project's strengths and difficulties.

## Developing a community-performance event about shoes, feet and dance

Shoes bear the creases of our life.[12]

*Best Foot Forward* (*BFF*) was an eighteen-month series of workshops and performances that involved a partnership with the Melbourne-based Diana Ferrari Shoe Factory as well as with members of the local community. It was conceived around images of shoes and feet,[13] and its focus was on dance and movement.

Two local choreographers: Vanessa Case and Christos Linou co-directed the project. Christos was keen to collaborate with local-industry workers, and developed a fruitful partnership with the shoe factory. Vanessa focused on the local schoolchildren, including special-needs students from the Preston Special Developmental School. Christos and Vanessa shared a desire to develop contemporary-dance practice within the Darebin area.

The project consisted of a number of performances generated in a variety of venues through movement, visual art, music, film and storytelling. The aim was to create links between people, regardless of their culture, abilities and age; the age range was six to eighty years. The developmental objectives of promoting friendship and creative expression were supported throughout the project.

The project period was brought to a grand conclusion at the PCLC on the twenty-sixth and twenty-seventh of November 1999, when *Stepping Out with Your Best Foot Forward*, directed by Christos, was presented. This final performance featured people in motorised wheelchairs, movement sequences, and personal stories. The themes of 'shoes' and 'feet' and of 'journeys, internal and exterior' were woven together.

In the following two lists, we summarise the activities associated with *Best Foot Forward* during 1998 and '99.

## A summary of the activities

### 1998

- A Toe in the Water: a choreographic workshop and dance classes
- *TOE*: a performance and workshops held during the Great Darebin Music Expo
- The First Step: workshops in art, reflexology and foot massage
- Footage: a workshop in choreography and Super-8 filmmaking
- Preston Special Developmental School workshops: art making of individual 'shoe' totem poles by each student
- Foot Where?: banner making for people who had a disability
- Foot Where?: movement workshops for people who had a disability
- The Kick Start launch at the Darebin Festival: performance of the *TOE* choreography
- The Walking Together parade at the Darebin Festival: a float in the shape of a large shoe
- The Circle of Rhythm and Dance at the Darebin Festival: presentation of the *TOE* choreography
- At Edwardes Lake, a local ground used for the Darebin Festival: a roaming performance of the *TOE* choreography
- The Shoes with Soul exhibition: presentation of Robyn Shannon's visual artwork
- The '98 Xmas Celebration: performance and presentation of the first six months' work

**Figure 5.2** A movement sequence from the final performance of *Stepping Out with Your Best Foot Forward.*

### 1999

- Monday-night workshops: drop-in classes in movement, storytelling and music
- Dance workshops for primary-age children: dance classes and banner painting using the feet
- KUCA and kindergarten workshops: dance classes and banner painting using the feet
- Preston Special Developmental School workshops: classes in dance and music
- Senior-citizen dance workshops: movement classes for people between the ages of sixty and eighty, with Bronwyn Ritchie
- The Shoemaker exhibition: presentation of Diana Ferrari employee Terry Doyle's portraits of the shoe factory's employees of the month
- The Putting Your Foot in It exhibition: six banners made during previous workshops
- Red Shoe Day: performance and workshops in which Vanessa Case concluded her role as community artist
- *Ankle High*: an event that included dance, visual arts, storytelling, film and shoemaking, held at the Diana Ferrari Shoe Factory
- The street parade at the Darebin Festival: a 'walking' entry of live percussive musicians
- *Stepping Out with Your Best Foot Forward*: the final performance

# Conceiving the project

The impulse for undertaking the *Best Foot Forward* project and forming its artistic viewpoint arose from a series of meetings. Christos Linou was interested in whether any contemporary-art maps were being made in Melbourne's northern suburbs. He approached the City of Darebin, and the council staff members directed him to Darebin Dance Link, an informal group of ten dancers who were dedicated to raising the profile of dance in the area.

> The dance profile had to be raised in Darebin. The theatre side of the performing arts is quite well supported and encouraged. Several dancers were meeting, and Christos joined our group.
> – Dance Link member Vanessa Case

The impulse for undertaking the project also arose through convergence of three other factors:

1. The members of Darebin Dance Link were interested in obtaining rehearsal space and support for their focus on community and contemporary dance.
2. The PCLC's staff members were developing a reputation for helping isolated local artists to network with each other and for promoting the performing arts in the community. They were looking for a new artist to lead their next annual performance-making project.
3. Christos Linou had a strong desire to make a contemporary performance in collaboration with local-industry workers.

These three sets of concerns came together in *Best Foot Forward.* The following objectives were set for the project.

## The objectives

- To provide a cultural celebration of feet and shoes
- To suggest the diversity of Darebin's cultural communities and the relationships the members form through their work, dance and recreation
- To give the artists the skills necessary for them to include, in movement workshops, people who had a disability
- To establish a series of events in which the area's shoe history would be incorporated

- To form a partnership with a local shoe factory
- To present a quality, multimedia performance in the shoe factory

One of the project's key components was that a number of strategic developmental links were forged with the members of identified groups. In the following description of the project, we highlight four links that were forged in order to facilitate local people's participation.

## The four links

1. With industry workers
2. With schoolchildren and older adults
3. With people who had a disability
4. With artists

## Forging links with industry workers: the Diana Ferrari partnership

Historically, the shoe industry has been a major feature of the Darebin community's economic and social fabric. The *Best Foot Forward* arts-team members linked into this history by forming a partnership with the Diana Ferrari (DF) Shoe Factory. They related images of shoes, feet and journeys to this industry context, and used them as evocative starting points for artistic exploration.

The partnership had two major outcomes:

1. *Ankle High*, a performance by factory workers and other performers that was presented at the DF Shoe Factory and involved stories, film, movement and music

2. The Shoemaker exhibition, a display of Diana Ferrari employee Terry Doyle's portraits of the factory's employees of the month, which was presented in the PCLC's Art & Soul Gallery

I'm a northern-suburbs person, a Coburg person. One of my aims for contemporary arts, as a 'city-folker', is to network here in the northern suburbs. If there isn't any of this type of art, we need to create it, as well as an awareness of contemporary-art making. I'm also interested in taking performances to unusual locations.
– Christos

# Developing the partnership

Christos commenced his research by approaching the Australian Chamber of Manufactures, and was led to the Diana Ferrari Shoe Factory. At the time, more manufacturers were deciding to produce their goods offshore. However, DF's managers had decided to source 70 per cent of the company's shoes onshore. They'd constructed a new factory in the Darebin suburb of Fairfield, and the company had won international awards for its worker relations. The factory workers were members of onsite committees and were involved in making decisions for the company. They and the company's managers had developed mutually agreed-on principles and values.

Christos gained access to the factory because the company's human-relations manager, Charles Cutajar, was convinced that the project would be good for both the workers and the company's profile. DF was about to celebrate its twentieth anniversary, and *Best Foot Forward* became part of the year of celebrations. This is an example of how project partners can mutually benefit from the project. Although the partners had different reasons for coming together, through the project they were provided with a shared focus and a way to fulfil each partner's aims.

**Figure 5.3** The back of the T-shirt designed for DF's twentieth-anniversary celebrations: '20 years of comfort and style'.

It was necessary for representatives of the factory and the PCLC to develop a written partnership arrangement. Skilled direction was required for developing the arrangement. Christos convened a taskforce that consisted of Barbara Doherty, who's now the Regional Arts Officer (Victoria) and chairperson of Arts Access, and Brenda McDonald, who was experienced in mounting publicity and marketing campaigns. The four taskforce members developed and wrote a proposal for formally obtaining sponsorship. In the proposal, they outlined the benefits for both the major partners – the Diana Ferrari Shoe Factory and the PCLC – of forming a joint community-arts partnership based at the factory.

Through the project, DF was given media coverage, display opportunities at major events, the ability to display its logo and factory name on printed material, and the opportunity to address a community audience. In return, the *BFF* arts team requested access to and use of the factory within agreed parameters, off-cut materials for artworks, and interview time with work-floor employees.

Christos convened a joint steering committee through which representatives from DF and the arts team directed the project at the factory.

This group worked hard to clarify what our responsibilities were as partners in the project. The PCLC and DF, we were both in learning mode. Meanwhile, I met with Charlie Cutajar on a monthly basis and kept him updated about the project's progress.
– Christos

Christos attended the factory with arts-team member Liz Landray, who made audio recordings with some of the employees. The following passage is excerpted from the interview Liz conducted with employee of the month Bettina.

## *Bettina's interview*

*I've worked at Diana Ferrari for four years. I work in one of the bigger modules, which is a 'cut to box' module. You could be doing anything, right along the line. There must be six or seven stages along the machine side, so it's just 'go; go; go'. It's interesting, if you haven't seen 'cut to box', because you start with the clicker and the bit of leather, and you just see how it goes through, right through to the back, up to the end, and then in a box for the shops.*

*I'm on the final end that goes into the making, so I do the final stitching on a shoe. 'Toe it up': put a toe on it inside the stiffener, and then a stiffener in the back counter – the heel – and then size it in the sizes. Then they go out the making side. All the top part has been made, but it hasn't got the heel, sole or inner part yet. More than 500 pairs of shoes are made a day – all done and boxed, which is pretty good for twenty-two people.*

*Before Diana Ferrari, I worked for Footrest Shoes for more than twenty-eight years, so I've always been in the shoe trade.*

Using Super-8 film, Christos filmed a factory sequence he entitled *Footage*. The finished footage was used to back the two final performances of *BFF*, one at the factory, the other at the PCLC.

PHOTO: CHRISTOS LINOU

**Figure 5.4** Placing pairs of shoes in the sunlight in preparation for a film sequence in *Footage*, for the final performances.

## Developing the outcomes

### The Shoemaker exhibition

Meanwhile, Vanessa, as co-artist, had set in train The Shoemaker exhibition, a three-week display of DF employee Terry Doyle's portraits of workers who'd been awarded Employee of the Month.

> The Shoemaker exhibition developed into being the first public expression of our partnership with the factory. The factory's owner-director, Tony Kirkhope, opened the exhibition, which featured twenty portraits of DF employees of the month; the portraits were created by company employee Terry Doyle. Each honoured employee was interviewed and their story displayed with their portrait, together with their favourite DF footwear. A large cross-section of the community gathered for the evening opening: the artist and his family, a few employees, friends of the gallery, and interested community members. – **Vanessa**

## Ankle High

On the twenty-third of October 1999, more than 220 people and fifty participants gathered in the Diana Ferrari Shoe Factory's dining hall. Project participants had converted the facility to a performance space for the day in order to present the collaborative multimedia production *Ankle High*. Christos and the arts-team members produced the event, and some of the factory workers had specific roles. The arts-team members interspersed cameo spots with Super-8 film footage of the factory processes, ambient music and syncopated percussion that imitated the sounds of the manufacturing line.

In the first cameo spot, an apprentice shoemaker crafted a shoe on stage as she related her story:

## The apprentice shoemaker's story

*I went to a shoe-factory auction in Northcote recently. I saw how people who worked there personalised their work. These craftspeople had named their machines or brought Christmas decorations. They'd worked together for ten or twenty years as a team and knew each other really well. What were they doing now? I got really sad.*

*Here I was at the auction, looking for a bargain. It made me wonder why I was working to be a shoemaker . . . But this experience gave me a bit of history – it's more than making the shoe: I learn things to apply to my life; to use lateral thinking more to solve a problem; to be more truthful, 'cause no matter how you dress up, you can't get by in bad shoes very long. I also learned the importance of teamwork, of generations' working together to teach skills to people like me. I now put blood, sweat and tears into making a pair of shoes. That's what keeps me alive: I'm being creative.*

In another cameo spot, Marina Bistrin remembered her childhood dream of owning a pair of ballet shoes:

## Marina's story

*My mother went to buy me ballet shoes. She didn't have much money, but I was so excited when I got the package. I ripped it open . . . but they were the wrong sort. I wanted the ones with the hard toes, so you could go up on your tippy-toes, and arabesque and pirouette. I don't know if I even thanked her. She went away, and I sat there.*

*I put them on.*

*I took them off.*

*Then I thought,* Oh dear: egg cartons! *I ran down to the kitchen, got an egg carton, ripped out two cups, and stuck them in my ballet shoes.*

*And yes: I was up there, arabesquing; pirouetting; doing ballet – until they collapsed. They only lasted about five seconds!*

*Then I had another idea:* Picnic cups. *We had these little cylindrical picnic cups. I stuffed them in the toes of my shoes, and Yes! I was up there, arabesquing; pirouetting; flying as long as I could stand the pain – about five seconds.*

*But my pain tolerance grew better. I got up to twenty seconds, and between the long, cylindrical but painful picnic-cup dances and the shorter but more comfortable egg-carton dances, I had my moments of glory. They were blissful.*

The *Best Foot Forward* project was a great experience. I took my granddaughter to Red Shoe Day, and she had an absolutely wonderful time.
– PCLC staff member Kathy Beckwith

Diana Ferrari staff members and marshalls guided the audience members along the factory floor, past visual-art displays, such as mobiles of shoe off-cuts; a film-loop installation and recordings of employee interviews; and finally outside to a sausage sizzle, hosted by other DF staff members. Wandering musicians serenaded the guests, and face-painting artists entertained the younger visitors.

In the end, the collaboration worked, but industry and community arts are certainly two different cultures. The employees allowed me to film them, and Liz got her interview records. One worker and her son sang in the factory performance, and several workers' stories were represented. Other workers contributed to the performance day in a way that was comfortable for them: many were marshalls for the tour of the factory, following the performance. The people involved had a wonderful time. For some, they also showed their families where they worked, in the context of a fun day. – **Christos**

## Forging links with schoolchildren and older adults

Vanessa made fruitful links with local schoolchildren. She drew on her teaching experience when dealing with a variety of students, both primary age and special needs. She recalls some of the activities as follows.

I got involved in the Preston Special Developmental School. It was easy to approach the school because it had a history with the PCLC. I also developed a banner-making workshop with four Darebin primary schools. I used imaginary paint to teach dance, and then had the students actually paint their feet in selected colours and dance the routine on a canvas. The end results were very colourful. The five large canvases later became the backdrops for the Diana Ferrari and end-of-project performances, and now reside in the schools.

**Figure 5.5** Some of the schoolchildren who foot-painted a backdrop at one of Vanessa's workshops.

**Figure 5.6** The *papier mache* red stiletto used in the Red Shoe Day performance.

During this stage of the project, Vanessa was assisted at the Preston Special Developmental School by local visual artist Robyn Shannon. Robyn had each student create a piece of 'shoe totem' artwork, and we later exhibited the works at the PCLC's Art & Soul Gallery, under the title Shoes with Soul. Robyn also created the project's *papier mache* red-stiletto prop.

The culmination of Vanessa's work with the local schoolchildren was Red Shoe Day, held in June 1999 at the PCLC. Under Vanessa's direction, the primary-school dancers were showcased, together with the arts-team members. In the program, the more formal performances were interspersed with enthusiastically performed folk dancing and belly dancing. The event concluded with a rousing conga line of eighty participants laughing and sharing their dance routines.

> It was a wonderful exchange of music and dance for each other. I had originally worked towards staging a more traditional performance for an audience, but in fact it ended up being good the way each group interacted on the day – dancing their hearts out, feet flashing. I wish I'd fostered it that way from the outset.
> – Vanessa

During Vanessa's project year, she also worked with local senior citizens, retired church members, the children at a local kindergarten, and members of the Preston Uniting Church's after-school club.

**Figure 5.7** Some of the audience members during the performance.

PHOTO: GEORGE MIFSUD

## Forging links with people who had a disability

Both Vanessa and Christos had the professional–development objective of working with people who had a disability. During the project's early stages, Christos was approached by a representative of Leisure Action (part of Scope Victoria), an activities group for people who have a disability, to run movement workshops with its clients. A number of the clients used a wheelchair and were keen to be involved in the activities.

Vanessa and Christos led Foot Where? banner-making and movement workshops. The banners the participants made were displayed on a project float during the Darebin Festival parade. During the workshops, people who had a disability explored improvisation, storytelling and choreography. They created and performed several short pieces in *Stepping Out with Your Best Foot Forward*, the finale performance, which was presented at the PCLC.

For the final performance, *Stepping Out with Your Best Foot Forward*, Bill Hurley told his story:

**Figure 5.8** Two of the participants creating a banner during a Foot Where? workshop.

PHOTO: CHRISTOS LINOU

## Bill's story

I loved football with a passion. I asked my father and my mother for a football.

'I can't afford that,' they said. They weren't earning much at the time.

I wanted football boots. I was rapt when I finally got football boots. I was kicking football!

But I had two teachers at school: a Scottish teacher and a Greek teacher. The Greek teacher would say, 'Kick the goal. Kick the goal. You don't really play football.' The Scottish teacher – in brogue – would say, 'Kick the ball. Auch! You don't play football.'

I didn't like soccer. I played Australian Rules football – a real man's sport.

Times change. I had an accident. How can you play football in a wheelchair?

Then someone suggested wheelchair soccer. 'I hate bloody soccer!'

Eventually, I played a few games – and we wound up at the grand final! We won medals, and I was rapt!

**Figure 5.9** The finished banner.

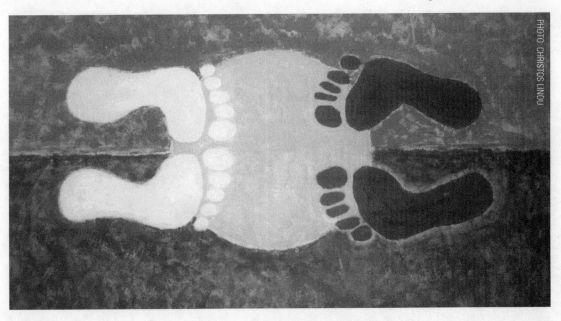

PHOTO: CHRISTOS LINOU

It took a considerable amount of advance planning to run the workshops – negotiating work time with the care-house staff members; ensuring that the participants were accompanied by a family member, carer or support-staff member; and booking the taxi or transport that each participant required.

We were all involved in a pretty intense and lengthy process. There were great long-term benefits for some of these participants, as well as for us. – **Christos**

## Forging links with other artists: developing a core group

Another one of *BFF*'s important features was a series of ongoing skills-sharing workshops for local dance practitioners and project participants. From these workshops, a core group of participants developed who performed in the three major performances and helped develop the ideas for the project. As a result, the project was given continuity across the months and various performances.

Terry Doyle recalls how he became involved in creating the portraits of DF employees of the month for the exhibition The Shoemaker:

**Figure 5.10** One of the pieces of artwork at the Shoes with Soul exhibition.

### Terry's recollection

*I was vacuuming among the machines at Diana Ferrari Shoes, when Andrew called me over. 'Hey, Terry, come and meet someone.' There was Andrew, with a stranger who was carrying a Super-8 movie camera.* How unusual, *I thought.*

*That's how I first encountered Christos and the* Best Foot Forward *project, and the Preston Creative Living Centre. 'An art project meets the footwear industry': here was a chance to exhibit the portraits of the Employee of the Month scheme, as I was secretly hoping and planning – somehow, in a proper gallery, somewhere.*

*Those portraits, in watercolour pencil on paper, were an important dream. I wanted to do a series of portraits of people who were, sort of, chosen at random: ordinary people who wouldn't necessarily expect to have themselves painted. And the discipline of having a regular gig that went on relentlessly shook my ideas up a bit. It went on for a total of thirty-two months, and I feel I produced an interesting document of Australians in industry.*

It's amazing, when you start talking about shoes: people always have stories to tell you about their shoes. I like the eye-catching aesthetic of stilettos, but I don't wear them.
– Robyn Shannon

## An evaluation of the project

We're able to articulate the following strengths and difficulties as a result of an evaluation undertaken by the project's managers, key artists and participants.

## Strengths

1. The PCLC gained a broader network and context.
2. Each key artist focused on the project's aspects that were best suited to his or her talents and experience, and simultaneously pushed the boundaries of his or her learning and artistic skills.
3. The PCLC enjoyed a considerable amount of promotion and publicity as a result of the project.
4. The participants became more confident, and the level of their self-esteem and creative skills was raised.
5. The performance outcomes were successful because we'd negotiated an effective partnership with the Diana Ferrari Shoe Factory.

6. The *Footage* film has had subsequent screenings in various experimental cinemas, including three film-festival screenings.
7. Leisure Action initiated approaching the PCLC on the strength of the centre's reputation for inclusiveness and creativity.

## Difficulties

1. Because a veritable plethora of ideas was generated as a result of the chosen theme – 'shoes, feet and dance' – we were over-ambitious in selecting too many aspects to focus on.
2. Both the PCLC's staff members and the artists under-estimated how important it is to have specialist training in order to work with people who have a disability.
3. We learned that the arts and industry cultures differ from each other. Whereas during the arts processes the participants adopted an exploratory and personally expressive approach, in the factory environment the workers were often nervous about revealing themselves.
4. Because of the project's multi-faceted nature, we found it difficult to draw a coherent group of performers together.
5. Christos and Vanessa experienced difficulties in integrating their separate visions as co-directors.

In the case of *Best Foot Forward*, the partners included the artists initiating, developing and directing the idea; the host agency providing a support network and guidance; the local partner providing primary material and opportunities for outcomes; and members of the community having individual stories for shaping a rough outline of the project's material. I think it's important to note that in the Community Performance Making Program, the catalyst was provided for all these different people to cross paths.
– **Arts-team member Liz Landray**

## The overall impact

In *Best Foot Forward*, we ventured into new territory by forging links with industry: new territory for the two key artists, the PCLC and the City of Darebin. In our effort to bring together two cultures – commercial manufacturing and artistic creativity – we expended a lot of energy. In both cultures, people make a social contribution – but will the cultures 'wear' together?

For the people involved in the cultures, the project's overall impact was mutually beneficial. However, from our perspective, we had much to learn about how to negotiate industry access, worker interest, artist prerogatives, and the PCLC's all too finite limits in terms of time and funding. The two key events: the industrial collaboration *Ankle High*, held at the factory, and the exhibition The Shoemaker, held at the PCLC, were received with delight by their audiences.

During the project, people of varying physical ability were given an opportunity to create art together. Many people who saw *Stepping Out with Your Best Foot Forward* will cherish their memory of sports player Bill Hurley speaking movingly about the impact of his injury, and of young participant Leanne Sheriff smiling radiantly in her wheelchair as she danced with Christos under laser lights.

Over the project's eighteen-month life, many people became enthusiastically involved. People expanded and shared their artistic skills, and established and valued their relationships.

Dad took us to see the dance night because Vanessa does artwork with the students at his school . . . Vanessa and Liliana danced *slooow*, and they used lots of feeling, and you could see that they loved to dance and prance around. As they danced, it was like they were telling a story about each other without using many words. I really want to go again.
– Young audience member Joe

## 'Employment and nurturing': a reflection from Vanessa

*In 1998, my needs were to establish myself as a* bona fide *artist – both as a performer and as a community artist; to have support and mentoring in relation to the skills required in these roles; to raise the profile of dance in Darebin; and to expose people to new possibilities if they mightn't have been involved in artistic practices.*

*By 1999, having had eight months of employment and nurturing during* Best Foot Forward, *these needs had changed. By then, I was working to become more independent and to encourage more participants who might only be interested in the project's processes, not its performance outcomes.*

*By the time my role in the project had concluded, I'd gained a higher profile and become better able to establish links with other artists. I'd also been given a context in which to connect to the wider-community dance field.*

**Figure 5.11** Vanessa and Christos.

PHOTO CREDIT LEADER COMMUNITY NEWSPAPERS

## 'A softer person': a reflection from Christos

*During the project's early stages, at that stage in my career, I wanted to develop my skills in public relations and in facilitating activities for people who have a disability. I also wanted to establish links with industry via a community-arts project, and to break down barriers between contemporary-arts practice and community arts.*

*Later on during the project, I found that the PCLC administrators and the participants in the Community Performance Making Program acted as a base for me to enable these experiences to take shape.*

*I feel I achieved my goal of creating a credible arts event in an industrial setting. It was a hard area, in which the culture was entirely different. I learned that numbers aren't always the true measure of results in community arts, and that the learning you gain during the process can be more important than attaining the project's original aims.*

*For me, there were lots of benefits. I was both a community artist and a manager. You 'walk the walk' according to who you're linked with.*

*Through the project, I went on an artistic exploration of story and abstraction that I probably wouldn't have gone on if I'd been working on my own contemporary-dance piece.*

*And the length of time: I wouldn't otherwise have had that luxury of having the long time involved in the process. I think that was the advantage of the project, both for performance results and for me and the other participants artistically.*

*The project changed me: it made me a softer person.*

# Part Two

PHOTO: KYLA JANE HUNT

## Taking care of business

# 6  Coming of age

In this shorter chapter, we look forward, find themes and recognise the potential that exists within the Community Performance Making Program.

## The journey's three stages: gathering, deepening, and entering into new territory

By 2000, the Preston Creative Living Centre had travelled quite a way down the track of community-performance making, having been home to three distinctive and dynamic projects. In each project, a specific action had been initiated in the Preston–Reservoir community.

- The first project, *Once Upon Your Birthday*, gathered people into the performance-making process and into the PCLC.
- The second, *Spinning, Weaving: Trees and Songs*, deepened the creative process and extended the audience.
- The third, *Best Foot Forward*, moved outwards, making links with industry and schools.

If a common thread runs through these projects, it's storytelling.

Each project dipped into the sea of people's stories. Each time, everyone involved was taken aback by the abundance, the detail and the poetry of the stories and by their power to communicate with audiences. The themes were big, rich and inclusive. Each time, though, the performance form – the dance, the music and the theatre – was utterly different.

**Figure 6.1** The main images used to promote the three projects.

Over the years of this work, the focus of the Community Performance Making Program has shifted and matured. During the early stages, the focus was on individual projects, whereas later, the work developed into an ongoing program that had its own integrity and life. This growth has involved both continuity and change.

In community cultural development, one of the dilemmas that community artists and organisational managers encounter is how to engender sustainable social change through one-off projects that necessarily have a limited life span. Because the PCLC hosts a project each year, evaluation of the previous project informs the aims and structure of the next. Over time, the PCLC has created a developmental context through which the community members' and artists' work is supported and strategic thinking is made possible.

For example, when the participants evaluated their experience in *Once Upon Your Birthday*, they said that they'd wanted a longer creative process as well as more time to rehearse and to get to know each other. As a result, it was recommended that the second project – *Spinning, Weaving: Trees and Songs* – be a smaller-scale project, have a longer rehearsal period and include a greater amount of artistic control for the participants.

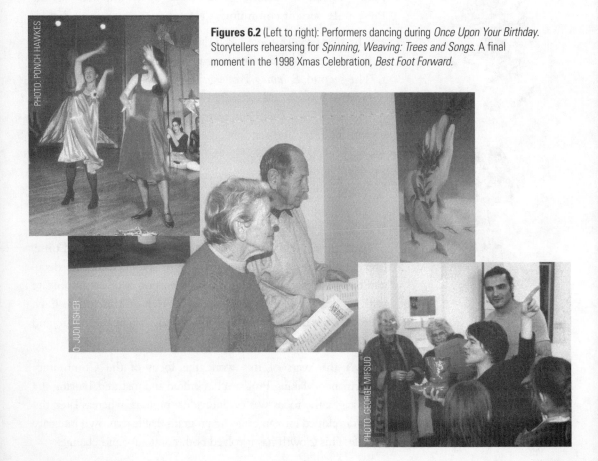

**Figures 6.2** (Left to right): Performers dancing during *Once Upon Your Birthday*. Storytellers rehearsing for *Spinning, Weaving: Trees and Songs*. A final moment in the 1998 Xmas Celebration, *Best Foot Forward*.

PHOTO: PONCH HAWKES

PHOTO: JUDI FISHER

PHOTO: GEORGE MIFSUD

As each project unfolded, it emerged that the process is every bit as important as the 'product'. When the participants evaluated *Spinning, Weaving: Trees and Songs*, they recommended that the third project – *Best Foot Forward* – have a longer process. As a result, it was possible for the PCLC to forge community connections over a longer timeframe.

Another aspect of the program's growth has been continuity in, and development of, the artists and community members across the projects. Bagryana gained her first community-theatre experience in *Once Upon Your Birthday*. After that project, she returned to direct the next, *Spinning, Weaving: Trees and Songs*. Marina Bistrin was a participant and group facilitator in *Once Upon Your Birthday*, and became a member of the core arts team in *Best Foot Forward*. Several participants from the first two projects – and from other PCLC projects – returned as either project participants or members of the core arts team in the third project. This transfer of skills and leadership is a very constructive outcome.

The program has been established as part of the area's cultural life and has become more accessible to direction from community members. As local people and organisation representatives get to know about the work, see its potential and acquire skills, it becomes possible for them to bend the work to their chosen ends, to initiate themes and projects, and to make the work more and more their own.

These goals are consistent with the meaning and intention of community cultural development as being a process in which community members proactively explore and express their identities and determine their priorities for the future.

The PCLC's presence in the community on an ongoing basis is central to the projects' long-term impact. Relationships and interests initiated during a project don't have to end because the project has concluded: the PCLC provides a focus for ongoing networks and activities through which the projects' benefits are extended and deepened.

We hope that in Part Two of the book, we provide grist for discussion and helpful information for people who are considering generating a performing-arts initiative in their community or organisation. First, we discuss some pointers to success at each stage of the project blueprint we've introduced in Chapter 2. Second, we highlight some possible pitfalls and provide some suggestions for avoiding them. Third and finally, we discuss how to manage your project both organisationally and financially. We include overall-management checklists, along with detailed information and/or useful references in areas such as contracts and fees, copyright, and budget development.

# 7 Trial and error, and the getting of a modicum of wisdom

In this chapter, we move step by step through each of the broad community and creative processes introduced in the blueprint in Chapter 2: the projects' origins, conception, processes, outcomes and evaluation. We've drawn on the experience of all three projects to discuss some of the questions and issues raised at each stage.

## Step 1: Origins

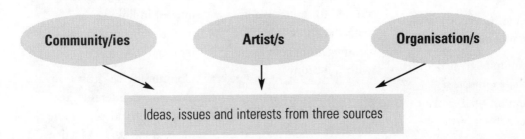

Figure 7.1 Blueprint: origins.

The PCLC's projects are grounded in the context of the Preston–Reservoir region. They're collaborations between three partners: community members, the PCLC and local artists. They originate in each of the three partners' aims, resources and priorities, as summarised, for our three projects, in Table 7.1, on page 76.

**Table 7.1** The partners' aims, resources and priorities

| *Once Upon Your Birthday* | *Spinning, Weaving: Trees and Songs* | *Best Foot Forward* |
| --- | --- | --- |
| The Preston–Reservoir region had a documented lack of arts opportunities.<br><br>Local artists felt isolated in the region.<br><br>The PCLC needed to raise its profile in the community.<br><br>Community artist Beth wished to initiate a community-performance project about birth.<br><br>Local people responded to the idea strongly and positively. | The artists were committed to airing older people's stories and to creating cross-age dialogue.<br><br>PCLC staff members wanted to strengthen links with the church congregations associated with the centre.<br><br>Migration issues were relevant to Preston–Reservoir residents, and the region lacked cross-cultural links.<br><br>Community artist Bagryana wanted to initiate a community performance based on her experiences of migration and love of stories.<br><br>Community participants wanted to be engaged in a longer, more intensive creative process than had been offered in *Once Upon Your Birthday*. | The PCLC aimed to form links with new sectors of the community.<br><br>Community co-artist Christos had a long-term interest in linking performance making and industry.<br><br>Community co-artist Vanessa was interested in developing and networking the region's dance practice and dance artists.<br><br>The Diana Ferrari Shoe Factory responded positively to the idea of hosting a performance project. |

Each project involves a judicious and creative combination of the current interests, needs and skills of the three partners – the community participants, the host-organisation staff members and the artists. The first step is to identify these various interests. To do so, representatives of the three groups have to talk, think, reflect and talk again.

Developing a project concept through which these various interests are honoured, integrated and balanced is certainly a creative act of its own. This kind of creativity is perhaps unique to community-arts processes as opposed to individual-arts processes.

## Questions, issues and points of learning

There are three key points here:

- The project designers need to take into account the major partners' current concerns and aims.
- Different but complementary aims of the participants, host organisation and artists can be furthered simultaneously during the project.
- When the partners identify their shared values, they find it easier to collaborate, and have a stronger sense of purpose.

Any of the three partners can provide the project's initial impetus. However, in our experience, the early stages were carried more by the artists and PCLC staff members, and the later stages were owned and driven by the community participants.

As community members become familiar with the process involved in generating a project, it's likely that they'll form their own initiatives and direct their own involvement. An example of this development is Leisure Action's involvement in *Best Foot Forward*.

That's where the metamorphosis was for me: I was an artist before I started the project, and the organisation was already there, but by the end of the process, the community members were completely involved. People become motivated and activated, and that's part of the incredible relationship of the work.
– Bagryana

# Step 2: Conception of the project

Ideas for a project can be developed in lots of ways. However, we found it very helpful to develop a clear project concept at the beginning of the project in order to guide action and provide a shared focus for everyone involved. The areas that were most useful to include in the initial project concept are flagged in Figure 7.2 and outlined in Figure 7.3.

Community
Story
Place, timeframe, budget and funding
Agreed action plan
Agreed expectations
Agreed aims
Project team

**Figure 7.2** Blueprint: conception of project.

## ✓ Checklist: project concept

1. **Community**: Have we clearly defined the project's target or population?

2. **Story**: Have we developed a succinct and inspiring account of the project for use as a crucial form of communication so we can involve people in participating, providing resources and so on?

3. **Place, timeframe, budget and funding**: Have we been clear but flexible in making decisions about aspects such as venue, timeframe, projected numbers of people involved, budget and resources required?

4. **Agreed action plan**: Have we formulated an action plan for finding the resources?

5. **Agreed expectations**: Have we reached agreement about the project's outcomes so we can focus the work, provide a base for evaluating the project and prevent the collaborators from misunderstanding each other?

6. **Agreed aims**: Have we reached agreement about the project's quantitative aspects, such as numbers of people involved in any aspect, as well as about the quantitative aspects, such as the quality of the relationships forged as a result of the work?

7. **Project team**: Have we established a small creative team – including the community artists – the members of which are the project's core?

**Figure 7.3** A checklist of the major areas to consider in developing a project concept.

Let's take a moment here to correct an impression we might be creating. Despite the fact that we're recommending orderly lists of aims and a clear project concept to you, much of the process of working on a community-performance project is about discovering a creative path through chaos.

For example, only two people might turn up for a meticulously planned workshop, or a group that's central to generating ideas and energy might drop out, for reasons that have nothing to do with the project. Conversely, one incidental conversation might lead to a whole new understanding of the content or to an offer from someone to make twenty costumes! People might suddenly reveal skills, insights and ideas that prove to be crucial to the performance. The creative process is a bit of a 'wild thing': unpredictable, but bountiful.

Paradoxically, it's because of the organic, improvisatory nature of this work that a clear project concept is so important and useful. We understand the project concept as being a mutually agreed-on action plan for the project. It contains the landmarks that make it possible to take the unexpected journeys that bring the project to life but through which everyone is able to keep on track together towards the project's aims.

In developing the project concept, we found that we needed to engage in two related streams of thinking:
• community-development aims
• artistic aims.
Early in the process, the most formative question is probably:
• Who is the community in this project?

And hot on the heels of this question come questions such as:
• What will this community gain?
• What links will be forged, and what experiences will be engendered that will be of enduring value?
• What skills and capacities might we foster among community participants and artists?
• Will the project involve groups that are disadvantaged in terms of their access to arts experiences?
• Will pre-existing community groups be linked with each other?
• Will new groups be created that are focused on the project's work?
• How will this short-term activity connect with and be sustained by ongoing networks in the community?

> If I were working with elderly migrant women, the project would be one thing; if I were working with women who had a history of violence, it would be quite another – and working with a group of Islamic women would be a different project again.
> – Bagryana

It's in asking key questions such as these that strategic thinking is promoted, whereby the benefits that flow from the work can be optimised.

In the past, in many community-arts initiatives the aim has been to foster links within specific groups, such as older adults who have a disability or unemployed young people. According to current thinking, it can be equally important to take a 'whole community' approach and forge cross-group links between disparate individuals and groups.

In *Spinning, Weaving: Trees and Songs*, for example, we aimed to create cross-age and cross-cultural dialogue. We achieved this aim by bringing people of various ages and cultural backgrounds into the PCLC to work together in a creative process through which opportunities for profound communication were offered. In *Best Foot Forward*, we linked the shoe factory and the PCLC, that is, industry and the arts. To facilitate the linking, artists were brought into the factory and factory workers into the PCLC as a result of the project activities. It's through the pattern of activities within a project – who works where and with whom – that the parameters are set for what community development is possible.

When a project is being planned, these community-development questions exist in intimate dialogue with artistic questions about theme, form and process. Again, the 'Who?' question is crucial.

Clearly, the character of a performance project is utterly different according to who its creators and performers are. The themes of the performance must matter to the people involved. In our projects, people were invited to participate in a performance-making process in which a specific area of human experience – birth, family trees or journeying – would be explored. Because life themes and issues attract people who care about them, each project's thematic content had a role in defining the project's community.

In *Once Upon Your Birthday*, for example, because the focus of the project was on experiences of childbirth, it was relatively easy to form the project's community. A lot of people are passionate about birth; it's a clearly defined point in people's lives, and people congregate around organisations and resources associated with it.

For us, a performance project's artistic content has to:

- matter enough to the community members for them to engage in the project
- have scope for a process of discovery and articulation of individuals' 'knowings', experience and values
- contain a stimulating focal point for the arts-team members
- 'give voice' to aspects of the life of the community that are otherwise unheard, unarticulated and unrecognised.

Although either artistic interests or community-development initiatives might be the project's early focus, ultimately both factors have to be integrated in the project concept and have to 'feed' how the project evolves on an ongoing basis.

In each of our projects, the original project concept emerged during pre-project discussions between Judi and the artists. We wrote funding applications, defined the project's aims, clarified the role of the artist/s, and consulted the members of the PCLC's staff and the community.

In many ways, this collaborative process undertaken between the artists and the host organisation – with input from the wider community – was each project's first act of creation and was crucial to making the projects happen.

## Forming the project's core arts team

Unless a project involves only one artist, one of the most significant decisions you have to make is who the members of the core arts team will be. Usually, they'll be the paid workers. The team might comprise all artists or include people who have another role, such as a community-development worker, a publicity or administrative helper, a person who has knowledge about the local area, or a person who has expertise in a specific technical area. What type of team you need depends on what skills and support from other sources you have access to, and what's necessary for the project to be successful. It's sometimes possible to find people, for example council arts or cultural workers, who can fit their role in your project into their existing job description. These contacts can be invaluable.

If you're not a member of the community or group you'll be working with, it can be very helpful to include someone from

We worked with making movement vignettes around simple stories. For me, a good creative process is when we can draw out people's own skills and interests, and exchange our own. When people find ways to shape movement, they can look back on it and see their own input, which is terrific learning.
– **Community co-artist Christos, *Best Foot Forward***

that community or group in the arts team. As well as the specific skills that this team member brings to the project, he or she will be able to help you access and understand the people you'll be working with.

It can sometimes be tricky to make a clear distinction between the project's paid workers and volunteers. For example, when should a volunteer who's gained skills in a number of projects become a paid team member? Would it be appropriate to pay a community co-ordinator who's part of the target community? Should cultural-dance groups be paid for their performances whereas other performers participate on a voluntary basis?

There are no 'pat' answers to these questions. However, the thinking behind the policy you choose probably has to be both *strategic*: 'What skills are critical to the project's success?' and *ethical*: 'Is it fair and equitable to distribute the funds in this way?' Once you've arrived at a policy for the project, be consistent in implementing it.

## The timeframe

As the project shifts from the conceptual to the action stages, a clear timeframe for the events becomes a crucial organisational and communications tool. To develop a timeframe for the project, you need to envisage what steps have to be taken in order to bring the project to fruition. As the project gains momentum, the timeframe becomes both a checkpoint and a clear focal point for everyone involved.

**Figure 7.4** Blueprint: the processes.

*Making links:* conducting research and making contact with the community
*Making performance:* involving the community in the process and rehearsing

# Step 3: Research and community contact

Each of our projects began with a research period in which the artist/s explored the project's themes in the target community by organising interviews, discussions and workshops in order to discern how the project's ideas resonated in the community. This period was also a time for forging the links with people and groups through which the project is made possible. We found that this paid time for researching and contacting the community was invaluable in establishing a solid foundation for the projects.

## Questions, issues and points of learning

It's worth noting that although in our projects it was the responsibility of the project artist/s to invite people to participate in the project activities, this won't always be the case: the responsibility might be taken by staff members of the host organisation, individual people initiating the project, or a cultural planner. This work requires many hours, a creative approach and a certain unflappable determination!

For us, one thing that emerged strongly was how important it is to make personal contact when you're inviting people to become involved in project activities. Although newspaper coverage and flyers were important for giving the projects credibility and profile, they were rarely the sole source of people's involvement.

The phone became the centre of it: I rang and talked, and rang and talked!
– Bagryana

It's therefore important to talk to people, to go to the places in which they congregate and talk, to offer them workshops, to invite people you already know, and to tap into people's networks. This is one of the places in which the project 'story' really comes into its own. We found two effective ways to invite people into projects: inspiring them by talking about the project's potential, and offering workshops in people's familiar contexts.

**Figure 7.5** Bagryana Popov, on the far right of the photo, and Ilka White, second from left, discussing memorabilia with church members and local residents Elsie Gibbs and Marjorie Hansen; in the background, community participant Harold Osborne is working the loom.

# Step 4: Creative processes and rehearsal

Finally, as a result of the planning, research and fundraising, the space is prepared, and the artists and community participants can come together to create the performance. It's time to undertake the creative processes and rehearse: to make, dance, write, sing, paint, perform, listen and argue. The ideas of the project are about to come alive through people's creative engagement with artistic forms and with each other.

You can't make rules about creative processes: they wonderfully defy categorisation and prediction. However, we discovered that in community-performance making, the participants and the artists undertake at least three key processes: re-valuing, connecting and creating.

## Re-valuing

People engage with the project's ideas at a cognitive level – they discuss, listen and hear other people's views. They also engage with the ideas at an experiential level – through artistic exploration that involves memory, feeling and creativity. As a result of this multi-level involvement with the themes, people's values – for example about what birth means, or the worth of personal histories – are changed and articulated. The changes occur both on an individual level: personal journeys are taken and personal identities shift, and on a collective level: shared meanings are created and cultural values are challenged.

## Connecting

During the work, a space seems to be created for people to connect with each other in a special way, so that they're less caught up in concerns about status and competition than they are in most other social contexts. When we're absorbed in moving together or fired by co-creating a performance, we experience communion as well as a feeling of belonging and well-being. Flowing from this connectedness is the potential to create new networks that are of ongoing value for the community.

## Creating

People find it pleasurable and meaningful to create form out of their experience. When we co-create a performance, we forge a kind of communication that's uniquely ours, and when we perform, we take the communication to other people. This experience of co-creating, communicating and performing can be enormously stimulating, motivating and empowering.

## Questions, issues and points of learning

How can we optimise the flow of the three key processes of re-valuing, connecting and creating? It's at this point that the artist has a pivotal role as facilitator. Experienced community artists are able to structure experientially rich working sessions, and know when to lead and when to follow the community's lead. They're aware of their artforms' potential in community processes, and they take time to reflect carefully on the process as it unfolds. They ask themselves questions such as:

- What new 'knowings' and explorations are occurring?
- Who's making decisions about content and form?
- How might we honour participants' special needs and skills?
- How much control do participants have in driving the process?

We found that an effective way to pass on skills was to adopt the mentorship approach, whereby artists who are new to community processes work closely with experienced community artists. Although it's beyond the scope of this book to include a detailed discussion about facilitating artistic processes in the community, in Figure 7.7, on page 86, we include a community-development worksheet as a tool for grounding artistic processes in community-development principles.

> The process is about human beings and their creativity. That's the nature of community cultural development work: it's about nurturing, facilitating and encouraging other people to be creative.
> – Community artist Bagryana, *Spinning, Weaving: Trees and Songs*

**Figure 7.6** Four *Best Foot Forward* participants and their partners rehearsing a routine during one of the wheelchair workshops.

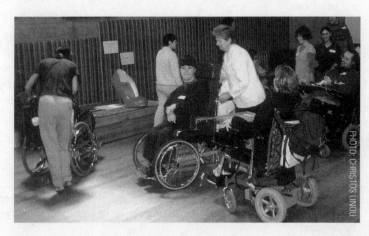

PHOTO: CHRISTOS LINOU

**Figure 7.7** The community-development worksheet.

# Community Development Worksheet[14]

Community development is a process of empowering people, both as individuals and in groups, to have more control over their life.

## The key principles of community development

- Humans are social animals.
- Collective identity and mutual responsibility are fundamental to human society.
- The experiences of each individual are shaped by the society in which he or she lives.
- Diversity within and among communities is a social asset.
- Inequities of power exist both within and among communities.

- Change is a constant.
- People are agents of social change.
- There is inherent value in the processes from which change can occur.
- Inequities of power have to be challenged, changed or eliminated.
- When change isn't possible in the short to medium term, this fact has to be acknowledged.

## Applying the principles

- ☐ Be realistic.
- ☐ Involve the relevant community members in assessing the needs: plan, develop, set goals, implement and evaluate.
- ☐ Have a blueprint or process to follow.
- ☐ Be open about the scope of community involvement.
- ☐ Share skills and provide opportunities for people to learn.
- ☐ Use appropriate and accessible language.
- ☐ Facilitate storytelling, discussion and debate.
- ☐ Draw attention to 'wins' and positive outcomes that occur along the way.
- ☐ Draw attention to what's happening in terms of process.
- ☐ Engage in resolving interpersonal issues.
- ☐ Value social time and social interactions.
- ☐ Talk about problems and stumbling blocks that occur.
- ☐ Be flexible.
- ☐ Validate having an opinion.
- ☐ Acknowledge that there might be more than one way to do things, and be prepared to do things differently.

- ☐ Build on existing structures and ways of working.
- ☐ Take a 'softly, softly' approach, unless there are good evidence and strong support for a 'boots and all' approach.
- ☐ Know and share, and learn from history: acknowledge that there are many histories.
- ☐ Acknowledge the costs that people will incur by becoming involved: time, money and social costs.
- ☐ Share responsibility.
- ☐ Acknowledge the diversity that exists within the group.
- ☐ Acknowledge people's grievances and have a process in place for dealing with them.
- ☐ Reflect, both as an individual worker and in a group.
- ☐ Acknowledge that you have power as a worker.
- ☐ Be aware of your own and other people's biases, values and agendas.
- ☐ Take risks.

In summary, *don't* try to change things overnight, to reinvent the wheel, to ignore history, to ignore powerful people, to take on all the responsibility or to focus on end results only. *Do* have fun, and be creative!

# Step 5: Outcomes
## Performing

Our projects' most direct outcomes were the performances. In each project, a new contemporary-performance work was created in which the performers' experience and values were expressed and new ground was broken in reaching audiences.

Each performance event had a different form, and through each form, specific outcomes were made possible, as summarised in Table 7.2.

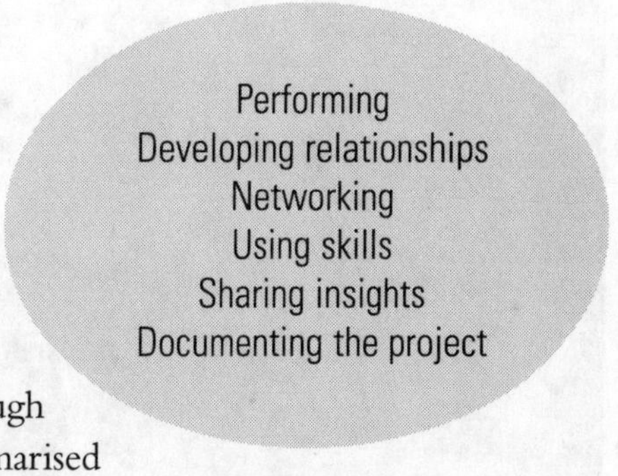

Performing
Developing relationships
Networking
Using skills
Sharing insights
Documenting the project

**Figure 7.8** Blueprint: outcomes.

**Table 7.2** The three projects' forms and outcomes

| Once Upon Your Birthday | Spinning, Weaving: Trees and Songs | Best Foot Forward |
|---|---|---|
| This was a multi-arts, one-off, site-specific, indoors–outdoors event.<br><br>This relatively large-scale type of performance was especially effective for creating a remarkable and high-profile event and for bringing together people from very different parts of the wider community. | This project had a short theatre season, and the performers and audience were in close proximity.<br><br>Through this intimate type of performance, a strong feeling of communication was created between the performers and the audience.<br><br>It was suitable for touring, and was reproduced for a second season, so that its audience was extended beyond the local area. | This was a series of workshops and performances.<br><br>Compared with the first and second projects, the focus in *BFF* was less on a culminating performance event.<br><br>Another priority was to conduct workshops and local events, as well as small performances along the way.<br><br>Because the project included these multiple outcomes, project activities occurred in a remarkably wide variety of settings, and a broad range of community groups were involved. |

**Figure 7.9** A participant on stage in *Spinning, Weaving: Trees and Songs.*

The possibilities for creating various types of performance are endless. The performance can, for example, be large scale or small scale; indoors and/or outdoors; formal or casual; site specific or transportable; presented in a theatre or non-theatre context; staged in the morning, afternoon or night; a stand-alone event or tied to a social or ceremonial function; a spectacle and/or involve audience participation; and a single artform or a multi-arts event.

Different forms of performance are associated with different processes and outcomes. Clearly, a street procession that features juggling and fire images; an in-theatre performance by local dance groups; and a night-time, outdoor, multi-media show will require different creative processes, attract different participants and audiences, and be the basis for different types of communication.

Determining what form the performance will take is a defining element of the project's life. The project partners are likely to choose the form in two stages. An initial image of the performance will develop during the concept stage. This image will be changed and honed once the creative process is underway. A fruitful question to ask might be:

• Through what kind of performance will the meanings and relationships that are central to the project be best framed?

Two important parameters are site and scale. Some potentially useful questions about each are listed as follows.

## Site

1. What relationship to place does the project have?
2. Will people better understand the performance in a theatre context, or does it carry meanings that belong either in a natural environment or at a landmark that's significant for the community?
3. Who are our audience members, and how can we make the work accessible to them?
4. In the eyes of the community, what status or credibility is conferred on our work because we're performing it on this site?
5. Does a pre-existing community event exist that we'd like to link our performance with?

## Scale

1. Are we aiming for a large-scale spectacular event in which we draw people from throughout the community together, or is the event to be smaller and more intimate?
2. Given the potential audience and the performers' needs, how many performances will be appropriate?
3. Will the audience see the event free of charge? If not, what would be a fair ticket price?
4. Will the event have components other than the performance, for example catering or an art exhibition?
5. What are our technical requirements for elements such as lighting and sound?
6. Can we access local people to provide us with the resources and expertise necessary for us to include these elements, or do we need to work with representatives from a professional company who are used to working in non-traditional contexts?[15]

Project partners often make these decisions about the performance's form intuitively and early on in the process. Although it's helpful to have an image of the final performance in order to inspire the process, it's also important to avoid getting locked into a series of unarticulated expectations that become burdensome in the developing project. We definitely found it worthwhile for all the project's partners to toss around the options. It's tricky maintaining the balance between aiming – and

**Figure 7.10** The stage layout for
*Spinning, Weaving: Trees and Songs.*

organising – for a specific kind of outcome and letting the performance's form evolve along with the creative process.

This tricky balancing act is related to a bigger question:

• How relatively important are the process and product?

It's easy to answer this old chestnut by simply affirming that process and product are equally important. In reality, though, in every community-arts initiative, you have to find this balance in your own way. According to one community-dance worker, it's about:

> . . . at all times trying to pay attention to the see-sawing demands of the participants' personal journeys and the quality of the art created as they [the participants] go. – **Sally Chance**[16]

There are people who would argue that the most meaningful aspect of community members' involvement in art making is their participating in the creative process: the experience, the doing, as opposed to the public outcomes. Although we agree that the process is the work's central element and has to be prioritised and protected, we view the process and the performance as being integrally connected. In a recent Australian study into the long-term benefits of community-based arts projects, the researchers found that long-term benefits ensued from both:

• having a personal feeling of being meaningfully involved
• being in a performance that the project's stakeholders highly value.[17]

In other words, the quality of both the process and the performance is important in achieving long-term outcomes such as fostering community pride, having a sense of identity, and developing skills.

**Figure 7.11** A whiteboard listing of the movement blocking for the choreography in *Best Foot Forward*.

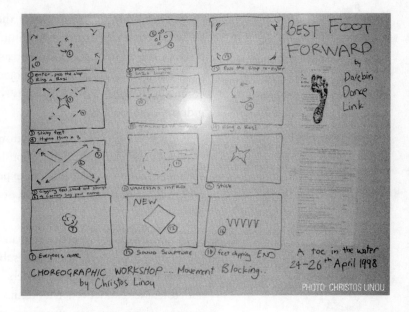

The anticipation of performing lends enormous energy, momentum and unity to the creative process. It's in performing that project partners find a public voice and that a new and unique piece of contemporary culture is given form. And as we've discussed, the performance can take a plethora of forms. Part of the project's creativity is to find a form that's right for the participants, the context and the audience.

A word of practical advice: because most of the performers are likely to be relatively inexperienced, it's important to make sure they're fully supported. They have to be clear about all the organisational aspects such as their warm-up times, the location of their change-rooms, their cues, and how their props are managed, so they can concentrate on and fully enjoy the performing experience.

## Relationships and networking

All the partners collaborating in a project forge new links and relationships. In our projects, we achieved cross-age, cross-cultural and cross-ability links in the region. Individual participants made new friends and formed ongoing associations. Local artists made ongoing connections with each other.

As a result of the performances, the PCLC has a higher profile and a different identity in its community. People know it to be a place in which unexpected and creative things happen, as well as a place of healing. Through the projects, the centre has established connections with new segments of its community, such as industry and the arts.

Relationships thrive in environments that are inclusive, respectful and purposeful. Relationships are deepened when the creative process involves positive experiences of sharing histories, revealing aspects of self, and encountering new artistic experiences.

In performance projects, a rich and safe environment is created for people from very different subcultures to encounter one another. Through these encounters, people build understanding and tolerance, and even friendships. Earlier in the chapter, we discussed how you can structure opportunities for cross-group relationships to develop into the project's activities. Cross-group contact can include semi-social occasions such as debriefing sessions – viewing a video of the performance is a popular example! – as well as working sessions.

Clearly, the potential for networks to have continuity is optimised when a community organisation in which people can gather is an ongoing presence. At the PCLC, we've provided a focal point for fostering the relationships that develop during our projects.

## Skills

In performance projects, a lively context is created for skills development. Some of the skills are specific artistic ones, such as stilt walking, weaving, writing, dancing and performing. Some are associated with teamwork, and with leadership and communication. The PCLC's project participants reported that they'd grown in confidence and self-esteem, and that they'd made gains in improving their skills in art making, communication, problem solving and teamwork.[18]

Project artists extend their skills in a new context. In our projects, we made it a priority to provide mentorship opportunities for local artists who were new to community performance. Mentorship requires more than proximity and the opportunity to be part of a project. The artist who's new to community facilitation needs tasks that are containable and achievable, time to observe and reflect, and directed supervision from experienced artists.

The opportunity for participants to develop specific skills can be a constructive entry point into a project. For example, young people might want to gain hip-hop dance skills, or, as in *Spinning, Weaving: Trees and Songs*, participants might be motivated by the opportunity to apply their weaving skills. Also, all communities are characterised by the presence of skilled people who'd value being given the opportunity to pass on their skills in a structured context.[19] Performance projects can be a context for this teaching and learning.

Because community-performance work is of a collaborative nature, people who have various types and levels of skill work closely together. A context is thereby created for accelerated learning in multiple directions.

**Figure 7.12** Community participant Maria Sapounas performing with a small child actor during *Best Foot Forward*.

PHOTO: CHRISTOS LINOU

# Insights

We've already discussed the new ways of being together and of creating meaning that are promoted in community performance. In each of our projects, the participants explored an area that isn't often given a public voice. The participants and audience members gained pleasure and shared insights as a result of clear expression of individual and community experience, values and understandings.

*Best Foot Forward* performer Maria Sapounas shared her personal story:

## Maria's story

*When I was a young girl of eight and a half years, back in Greece, my mother went to the post office and saw a poster saying you could be migrant workers in Australia. My mother put our names down, and we were accepted, so everyone was very happy.*

*Then we went to Athens to see my mother's family. My father took me to a shop to buy some shoes because mine were too old for the trip. We saw a pair called 'jelly-baby shoes'. They were purple and shiny – they were beautiful! My sister was screaming and crying 'cause she wanted a pair too, so eventually my father bought us both a pair.*

*Six months later, we arrived in Australia by boat. My father got a job quickly in a glass factory called ICI Glass, in Newport. It was really good. He worked there for twenty-five years.*

*About six months after we arrived, the Westgate Bridge collapsed, as everyone will remember. My parents went down to see the mess. After they fixed the bridge, a plaque was placed beneath the bridge with all the names of the workers who had died, and they were all Europeans.*

*It makes me sad when I go there now and see those names still, because my father died with glass particles in his lungs as well. It makes me want to dance the blues.*

PCLC staff member Kathy Beckwith shares the following reflection about *Spinning, Weaving: Trees and Songs*.

## Documenting the project

We documented *Once Upon Your Birthday* by photographing and videotaping the performance. We documented *Spinning, Weaving: Trees and Songs* by producing a seventy-page booklet of the stories, and by photographing and videotaping the performances. We documented *Best Foot Forward* by photographing and videotaping the performances, and collecting employee interviews and filming footage of people working on the factory floor. If funding isn't available to hire a professional photographer and video maker, the documentation can be adequately prepared on an amateur basis.

We found that we could extend a project's life and influence by having high-quality documentation. For example, the edited performance video of *Once Upon Your Birthday* and the booklet of stories generated during *Spinning, Weaving: Trees and Songs* have been well used in other settings such as artists' and organisations' training seminars, and in conferences conducted in the health and social-services sector.

We also found that having written and visual documentation was useful for reporting about the project to the people involved, for communicating about the work, and for subsequently preparing applications for project resources.

Evaluate.
Reflect.

**Figure 7.13** Blueprint: evaluation and reflection.

# Step 6: Evaluation and reflection

Immediately after each project had concluded, we set aside time for a comprehensive evaluation. Obtaining written and/or verbal evaluations of each stage of the project from everyone involved was central to this process, as summarised in Table 7.3.

## Table 7.3 How the three projects were evaluated

| Once Upon Your Birthday | Spinning, Weaving: Trees and Songs | Best Foot Forward |
|---|---|---|
| For the first performance event, we obtained written evaluations from fifty of the project's participants and from the project artists.<br><br>The evaluation was undertaken by the PCLC's managers and community artist Beth. | For the second performance event, we obtained a written evaluation from thirteen of the project's participants.<br><br>The evaluation was undertaken by a representative of the City of Darebin funding body, the PCLC's managers and community artist Bagryana. | For the third performance event, the evaluation was undertaken by the PCLC's managers, community co-artists Vanessa and Christos, and some of the participants. |

Evaluation and reflection begin when the project partners share their perceptions of the project and examine all the feedback received in light of the project's aims. Out of this process arises understanding of the project's strengths, difficulties and weaknesses. It was through this learning that we were better able to discern our future directions. It formed the basis of recommendations for future projects.

It's important to set aside time – and resources – for evaluation and reflection. If no thorough debriefing takes place and no opportunity exists for reflecting publicly or privately on the nature of a person's involvement – as a participant, an artist or a manager – people can feel acutely that the project remains unfinished. Evaluation and reflection are especially important for participants who need to be given permission to voice their experiences – positive or less than positive! – and for providing insight for planning future projects.

# 8

# Avoiding icebergs

In this chapter, we discuss some of the difficulties that can emerge during community-performance projects. We identify both the artistic and the organisational icebergs that can appear, and suggest some deft piloting strategies for avoiding a disaster of *Titanic* proportions.

## What are icebergs?

Viewed from a distance, icebergs are beautiful forces of nature, but encountered up close, they can be menacing potential causes of disaster. It's likely that everyone who's been part of generating a community performance has at some time or another felt the chill wind of an unforeseen problem that's about to surface.

Why do some projects fail whereas others succeed against great odds? Luck admittedly has something to do with it, such as when favourable conditions cluster together in perfect synchronisation: sufficient funds; proactive participants; the right community artists; an inspiring theme; appreciative audiences.

Organisationally and artistically, what contributing factors can cause the ship to sink? In Chapter 9, we discussed the critical factors, such as having adequate funding and realistic timeframes, which are essential for the project to be successful, and which can be anticipated and planned for sequentially. However, it's often the unanticipated problems that cause the most heartache, even for the most enthusiastic and prepared project partners.

These unexpected problems are the 'lighthouse' moments: the times at which it's necessary to seek help and advice from experienced people. At times, we found ourselves having to do this. At other times, we found ourselves being the icebreakers and having to negotiate ourselves, as an organisational and project team, out of the situation at hand. However, costs were incurred in terms of time, energy and artistic potential.

Although, in performance projects, it's necessary to resolve an iceberg or two, problems are almost always surmountable with goodwill and focus. Very rarely does a project get into full stride and then fail to go ahead. The problems encountered along the way simply become part of the learning curve in the project. In this chapter, Beth discusses artistic icebergs and Judi discusses organisational ones.

## Beth on artistic icebergs

When I was compiling this section, I decided to call on some of my friends and colleagues who were experienced community artists.[20] Speaking with these people, I gained a sense of the types of problem that occur relatively frequently, and some encounters resulted in some very funny conversations with other community artists about their favourite 'icebergs'.

One story about a good, hefty impediment came from the members of an arts team who'd worked in Broome to prepare for a moonlight performance on an offshore sandbar. The team members arrived for the performance to find a massive fishing vessel stranded smack-bang in the middle of the performance space. The canny and resolute project manager grabbed a loudhailer, and within half an hour the boat had been hoisted out of the way, borne on the collective shoulders of scores of good-natured beachgoers.

Unfortunately, not all problems can be solved as directly. As I sifted through the information other people had given me, and thought about my own experience, it became evident to me that the problems that had the strongest impact on projects were issues of relationship: relationship between artists and participants, collaborations between artists, and the relationship between the project and social and political forces in the community in question. For this discussion, I've chosen three examples in which to pick up on these issues. The other major theme that emerged from artists' stories was that of mismatched expectations between project partners. Judi will address that one in her discussion.

### 'It's just not working': when artistic collaboration seems to be a mixed blessing

One afternoon in June, six months into *Best Foot Forward*, Vanessa and Christos found themselves sitting in the PCLC's courtyard almost pulling each other's hair out. They felt they were adrift in a vast ocean of a project. According to Christos's compass, they needed to go one way: to focus strongly on the performance outcome in the shoe factory. Vanessa, on the other hand, was finding that her heart lay in the process of exploring dance with lots of varied groups. Tension had mounted around what the two key artists' roles were, and the two were unable to communicate candidly. Both of them probably felt like jumping ship, but they had to find a way forward in order to collaborate effectively.

In hindsight, Vanessa and Christos's dilemma makes some sense. In *Best Foot Forward*, Judi as the PCLC's director had unknowingly set up a situation of potential conflict by employing co-artists who had very different philosophies and approaches. Vanessa had come with a primary interest in inspiring people to enjoy the creative process, whereas Christos had come from the contemporary-arts scene, within which he'd been delivering creatively cutting-edge performances. He was focused on delivering artistically credible performances. Because of this difference in focus, it became increasingly difficult for the two artists to conceive of the project in a way they could share. An added difficulty they were facing was that neither of them felt that his or her stated job title, that is, Vanessa as artist-in-residence and Christos as production director, accurately reflected his or her actual relationship to the project.

When the reality of this difference in focus became evident and was articulated, about six months into the project's life, Vanessa and Christos's roles and work plans, along with the project's outcomes, had to be re-negotiated. The members of the Project Advisory Group and the rest of the members of the core arts team acted as mediators in the process.

In the resulting work plans, room was allowed for each person's main focus, but each person was also challenged to participate more fully in implementing the other's initiatives. For example, Vanessa was able to continue to encourage the primary-school students to focus on the creative process while also delivering an outcome – painted backdrops – towards the final performances. Similarly, Christos was able to concentrate his energy on the shoe-factory performance, but also participated in core-team workshops in which the aims were skills development and experimentation rather than a concrete end product.

Although I'm not wanting to be a 'Pollyanna' here, it's true to say that positive outcomes, for Vanessa and Christos as well as for the project, emerged from the resolution of the conflict. A constructive way forward was found whereby the two key artists produced separate outcomes with some shared goals and collaborated effectively on aspects of the factory event. Through this way of working, the *Best Foot Forward* team members were able to provide in-depth movement experiences for a wide range of people as well as a highly focused performance in an industrial context.

Artistic collaboration is a complex human relationship as well as a professional relationship, so there can be no guarantees as to outcome. For organisation representatives who are planning a project, it's probably a good bet to work with artists who have a proven track record of working together. There are loose groups of community artists who share a philosophy and practice, and who work in different combinations on projects. It's probably also wise not to try to impose specific titles on people, such as 'project director' or 'group facilitator', but to let the artists themselves define what roles they'll best be able to work in.

For artists who are looking to develop effective collaborative relationships, it might help to undertake short periods of work with potential work partners before embarking on a whole project, because much of the compatibility is 'in the doing'. For collaboration to be successful, shared creative processes and effective ways of communicating have to be evolved. It's also helpful for the partners to talk openly together about what working in the community means for them.

If you haven't collaborated very much with other artists as part of your training or in other contexts, you might find it useful to work with team members who are used to working together. They'll probably have developed effective communication strategies, such as regularly holding highly focused meetings in order to generate ideas, plan work and solve problems. They're also likely to have clearly defined roles and areas of responsibility that suit each artist, but they'll also view the whole project as being a shared endeavour.

### 'Hang on: whose truth are we telling here?'

It's the '90s, in Melbourne's outer east. I've been asked to direct a community performance at a small local hospital. I'm at one of those nerve-racking but inspiring first gatherings. I'd had no idea whether anyone would respond to my invitation – but here we are: several young mothers and babies, some people interested in local history, and some long-term residents, gathering to talk about a potential performance for marking the closure of the area's maternity unit. We chat animatedly about the possibilities. Then the iceberg hits: a red-faced, clearly angry man charges into the meeting and shouts a message, from the local Rotary meeting being held down the road, that what we're planning is wrong. *Wrong? How?*

It turned out that the Rotary man was right. The event we were planning was being sponsored by the local hospital. In it, we wouldn't be able to express the local community's substantial feeling against the closure or the unit staff members' devastation. We wouldn't be able to explore the closure's political context. After we'd spent time listening to people involved in each aspect of the situation, it became apparent to us that the suggested performance wouldn't be able to feature in any inclusive way the voices of the people involved. The performance would have been a Band-Aid on a community wound that was deep and unresolved. The project didn't go ahead. To my mind, this was the right outcome.

As a result of this experience, I realised that in setting up a productive and equitable project, a major concern was to establish, early on, who 'owned' the project: to understand the various interests involved and my own relationship to these interests. For me, the experience was confirmation of the importance of having a research and contact period at the beginning of a project. As we've discussed in the previous chapter, several strong logistical reasons exist for setting aside this period. However, in having this time, the people involved in the project are also given a crucial breathing space for hearing the various people's views and understanding the political context. This aspect is especially important when contentious issues are being explored. Having a depth of understanding of the issues is the necessary basis of being able to be clear and intentional about how our work contributes to community dialogue and social equity.

### 'Almost the full catastrophe': communication meltdown

It's the early '90s, in one of Melbourne's western suburbs. A show about young people, featuring 100 performers, is set to open in two days' time. Thirty young people, the show's entire youth contingent, arrive at rehearsal to say they're pulling out of the show. They say the director doesn't like them. Without them, there's no show.

It has to be said that although this is a true story, over a couple of decades of community-performance work, I haven't encountered as drastic a communication breakdown. However, I've included the story because the issues raised in it about artist–participant relationships are important. In this case, the young people's complaints carried considerable weight. The director was indeed often heard criticising the young people. She wasn't committed to working with the group, and had negative attitudes about teenagers. Furthermore, local-community workers who knew the young people and had been involved in the project's early stages had withdrawn when things seemed to be proceeding well. Therefore, the teenagers had no support for their involvement. Not surprisingly, they'd lost their motivation to participate, and they were angry.

For artists working with communities, the crucial point here is that it's ethically wrong to treat people simply as a means to an end in 'your' work. The work is about building relationships as well as about art. An artist seeking to work with people towards whom he or she holds negative attitudes is entirely on the wrong track. You're ethically bound to understand your own prejudices and limitations, and to respect the autonomy and personhood of the people you're working with. Otherwise, the work will become a form of exploitation of the community, and the result will probably be negative outcomes.

A secondary point is that in a project, it has to be part of someone's job description to support the involvement of participants, especially people such as teenagers, older people or people who have a disability, for whom issues such as transport can be problematic. It's often the case that the artist who's facilitating the group provides this support, but at other times, another team member might be the person who fosters participants' well-being in the project. In the case study outlined in this section, if this person had been on the alert, a crisis point probably wouldn't have been reached.

Third, had young people been included in either the core arts team or the Project Advisory Group, their interests would have been represented more fully in all aspects of the project. They would have 'owned' the ideas more fully and had a more proactive role in the project, and it would again have been much less likely that a communication breakdown would occur.

In case you're wondering what happened in this case study, a community facilitator was called in who listened to the teenagers' concerns. Together, they found a way forward, and the show went on.

At this point, I'd like to flag a somewhat related issue. If you, as a community artist, are considering working with communities that have a different cultural background from your own, you'll have to educate yourself about the culture. You'll have to be respectful and open while you're seeking to understand ways of doing things that might vary greatly from your own. For example, if you're a non-indigenous artist and you want to work with an indigenous community, you should not only carefully forge links with the specific community you want to work with; you should consult with a representative of an Aboriginal organisation in your state or territory and talk to any artists who are experienced in working in the area. You might also be able to locate printed resources. In the Northern Territory, for example, the Northern Land Council has published a guide entitled *Guidelines for Artists Wishing to Visit Aboriginal Communities*.

Forging exchanges between various cultural groups can be one of the most meaningful aspects of community-arts projects. However, these exchanges must be entered into with respect for difference and an understanding of issues pertaining to specific groups.

Perhaps a general point to be drawn from the aforementioned three stories is that one way to steer clear of icebergs is to make sure all the relationships that constitute the project are firmly grounded.

When working with communities, you have to be able to engage in and facilitate both artistic processes and human-relationship processes. This is part of what makes the work such a rich and interesting area for artists, and also, clearly, part of what makes it challenging.

A closing point: it's worth noting that there is sometimes a tendency for community artists to try to be all things to all people. This is especially so during a project's early stages. When you're working to make connections with people and to get a project up and running, it's tempting to answer 'yes' to every request or suggestion, even when the request falls outside the project's aims and parameters. It's not a good idea to be a 'yes' person! The project's resources, including your own time and energy, can easily become over-stretched, and the project can lose focus and direction. You might also inadvertently set up expectations that can't be fulfilled. It's much better to be clear about the project's aims and parameters, and to be generous and flexible within them.

# Judi on organisational icebergs

As the PCLC's director, I came to realise that the 'ocean' of arts-project management includes some quick team discussion and fast manoeuvring around obstacles. For example, for me, this management at the PCLC encompassed a community artist's project plan, community participants' personal realities, the PCLC's aims and objectives, various programs' priorities, and the committee of management's (now the board of governance's) policies – not to mention the principles of community cultural development work, and the influence of power and politics at any given time and in any given situation. All these aspects had to be aired and negotiated, sometimes simultaneously!

However, from the outset, I greatly enjoyed being involved as manager in the Community Performance Making Program, and found that the final results consistently exceeded my original hopes and expectations. Because of the strength of each project's friendships, performed work and artistic connections, I found that facing icebergs – and I encountered two or three – was a worthwhile occupational hazard.

The three issues I discuss in this section are accountability and expectations; the domestic issues of day-to-day arts management; and balancing the 'whole show' in order to deliver the maximum benefits for all programs, including the Community Performance Making Program.

### Informing each other: lines of accountability and levels of expectation

When Bagryana was our community artist, in 1997, and the project was concluding, she was invited to report directly to the PCLC committee of management. The invitation was given during the management meeting that followed the final performance of *Spinning, Weaving*. Bagryana inspired the committee members by stating how important the PCLC's Community Performance Making Program was. She wove dynamic images of the community's involvement, the depth of the friendships that had been developing, the exquisite nature of the theatrical piece, and the significance of the shared stories. In her report, she also made it clear to the committee that most of the program's artistic and organisational objectives had been achieved, and that many of the expectations of the local church, as the original sponsoring body, had been met.

Accountability is a major organisational necessity whereby the people involved are required to understand clearly established lines of communication. When people at all levels of the host organisation are able to communicate clearly and openly, the project can be managed effectively.

For the PCLC's committee of management (now the board of governance), Bagyrana's time of reporting was a positive moment in terms of the lines of accountability. Although, as director, I'd been reporting each month about how the project was progressing, the face-to-face experience of hearing Bagryana describe the stages in building the project, the enthusiasm she had for community-performance making in general and for the *Spinning, Weaving* project in particular, and the valuable results of a year's hard work, made an indelible impression on the committee members. Their sense of ownership of the program increased. Also, they had an opportunity to ask questions directly about aspects of the project, and the lines of accountability within the PCLC were completed.[21]

Opportunities for the artists and the host organisation to communicate directly are invaluable. Consequently, I suggest that as part of any new project's orientation, the manager clearly inform the new community artist of the lines of accountability that are in place within the organisation. He or she should also state where the artist's role in the accountability chain lies; for example, is he or she accountable to the board of governance via the director, to the committee of management via a verbal or written report, to a project-management team, and/or to the funding body or bodies via an acquittal report?

Accountability is also important because the people involved in any project or organisation carry expectations; that is, people have perceptions about what a project might be, has been or 'should' be. Although it's part of the human condition to have expectations, what these expectations are and how realistic they are have to be examined. It's necessary for the partners involved to communicate frankly and openly so they can find a reasonable match in terms of their expectations.

In the following summary, I provide an idea of the range of expectations that were met during our three projects.

## The committee of management

The committee of management expected the participants in the *Spinning, Weaving* project to meet the project's objectives in order to justify continuation of the Community Performance Making Program into 1998. The success of *Spinning, Weaving* therefore led to more project opportunities via both submission of more grant applications and community involvement.

## The congregation members

The members of the three congregations, who were the PCLC's originators, had varied expectations about the types of program to implement, the programs' impact on the community, the community's relationship to the congregations, and the intention that the PCLC return the benefit to the parish by becoming mostly self-sustaining.

## The PCLC staff members

At the PCLC, the staff members looked forward to experiencing the 'buzz' that would arise from the creativity of the arts-team members and the involvement of the community participants. As each community artist brought new interactions, the office-staff members, in particular, helped out in administrative ways. In 1997, Andrew Compton and Bagryana invited some of the men who were participating in the centre's behaviour-change program to participate in *Spinning, Weaving*. When it became clear that the men's involvement wasn't to materialise, Andrew himself became involved. In a small way, it was at this point that the programs' cross-fertilisation began to occur.

## The artists

In chapters 3, 4 and 5 of the book, we record some of the expectations held by the community artist/s and members of the core arts team: acquisition of new skills, extension of their art field and themselves, and staging of a quality performance at the end of the project. Some of these expectations are encapsulated in the following notes compiled from a project journal.

### The journal notes

What do we hope to get out of it? To see magic, communion, love; making a connection with new people from outside my circle of familiarity; sharing of history, making a little piece of new history; pleasure in doing it; for people to get a chance to express something new/old, to make something out of experience; for the piece to be delicate, well crafted, clean and finished; for the audience to laugh and cry, and 'know what that's like', to identify, to understand.

### The community participants

Some of the community participants viewed the project as being a learning space. Others sought a stage on which to share their stories and songs. Many enjoyed forging new friendships. Some came to weave the backdrop – and stayed! The reasons were as diverse as the people involved.

### Even me!

During the artistic creation, I always expect to encounter some surprises. Each year, I never knew what that 'gift' would be. However, my biggest organisational expectations were centred around our objectives for the program: enrichment of local people's lives by providing them with quality art in which their lives would be honoured, their stories would be shared, and understanding would be nurtured and increased, or some common ground would be found among the members of Preston–Reservoir's diverse cultural communities.

Everyone had expectations, some of which were shared and some of which were conflicting. Although not all expectations can be met – nor necessarily should they be – it's important that they all be communicated and 'put on the table' so they can be discussed, that decisions can be made, and that the outcomes can be managed for the good of both the organisation and the community.

How did we deal with these expectations? One way was to use the project's aims and objectives as a tool for aligning so many people's expectations with the project's parameters. Also, we held a number of forums for clarifying people's expectations, for example the Project Advisory Group, and face-to-face discussion between the artist and the committee of management or other levels of the host organisation. When known expectations are dealt with, the project itself can be viewed as being successful, in terms of both its craft and its context.

### 'We need more space and time': the domestic issues involved in managing community-arts projects

Ilka is in the kitchen, up to her rubber-gloved elbows in blue dye, stirring hand-spun wool skeins in a large, old soup pot, which she's positioned carefully in the sink. It's a big job, getting the yarn dyed for the five looms to be used for weaving the backdrop. Ilka has been at it all day, and is tired. However, she's yet to clean up the kitchen, put her utensils away, and find a safe place to hang and dry her freshly dyed wool. The members of the evening group will require access to the kitchen to make their evening cuppas. Ilka is frustrated, and longs to have a separate studio.

Competing requirements for a space, the space's condition and the host organisation's priorities: all contribute to the potential iceberg encapsulated in the words 'We need more space and time.'

As host organisation, the PCLC has provided workshop space, rehearsal rooms and office space for each annual Community Performance Making project as part of the organisation's in-kind support. However, the PCLC has also made room arrangements, which are annually 'signed off on', with other agencies and clubs that use the centre as their operational base. It's through these tenancies – of both community groups and professional organisations – that the PCLC earns a portion of the income that's necessary to balance its accounts and retain its programs. The PCLC solved this dilemma about spaces and rooms by tightly and strategically planning how the areas are used, and by requiring all users, including community artists, to book identified spaces and rooms. Administrative-staff members try hard to negotiate, well ahead, any variations in bookings, and in terms of access and time, the staff members and community artists have priority.

Some artists view room space as being a 'work in progress'. Differing expectations emerge when the room being used for the project is also a shared space for other purposes. In one host organisation, the staff members in this situation reportedly debated whether the organisation would ever again host an arts project, because they were very dissatisfied about the state of a shared room. Cleaning up, storage and security are therefore also issues associated with how a space is used.

Every host organisation will have its own parameters, terms and conditions for letting its space. Conflict can potentially arise when you're trying to accommodate the creative process within the room-booking structure and space-hire commitments that often exist in host organisations' community-used buildings. As in the case of participants' varying expectations, it's important that these parameters and terms be made explicit from the project's outset, and that constructive compromises be reached when differing purposes and priorities intersect.

## 'With the best of intentions': managing a community-arts project in the context of a whole organisation

One day, I arrived to find a fabric room divider blocking off the most recent art exhibition, Paternite, by Dom Violi. That was the first hint that I was facing an iceberg. Then Beth came to my office. It was just before rehearsals began for the performance of *Once Upon Your Birthday*. Beth said, 'I need to talk with you about the exhibition.'

Lynne Hyland, the Art & Soul Gallery's part-time co-ordinator, and I were working hard to establish the gallery as being a reputable space and exhibition area located in Melbourne's northern suburbs. A local artist who'd contributed formative input in the centre's early days had been invited to contribute to the gallery an exhibition based on the theme of 'fatherhood'. The exhibition became available for hanging to coincide with the performance of *Once Upon Your Birthday*, the celebration of pregnancy and birth.[22]

Although conceptually the two arts projects seemed to be a symbolic match, they didn't work together! Unfortunately, because naked men and fathers were depicted in the artworks, reactions were raised from all directions. Some church members were affronted by the nudity. Other people implied that the PCLC was weak with reference to addressing child abuse even though it was running a program for preventing family violence.

Beth, as the community artist, quickly conveyed to me that:

- the exhibition space was part of the performance area, so the audience members and participants wouldn't have a choice about viewing the exhibition
- if the exhibition remained, the trust that the centre had established with the project's community members – who came from many cultural and age groups – might be compromised as a result of our having introduced an unexpected and provocative element.

As the manager of the whole organisation, I had to find a way of balancing the needs of the people participating in two varying programs: the performance and the gallery. Although I strongly disagree with the idea that artistic expression should be censored, and wanted to preserve the artist's rights and interests, I accepted that the PCLC also had a prior (year-long) commitment to the community – the participants and audience members – via the performance-making project. It was necessary to reach a compromise so we could have a positive performance outcome. Lynne, Beth and I finally negotiated that the exhibition would be stored for the duration of the performing-arts sequence. Beth and I believe it's a credit to both our friendship and our sense of humour that we're relating this iceberg as co-authors years after it materialised!

As a result of this experience, I learned the following three lessons about arts-project management.

## Maintaining artistic integrity

Each artistic statement has its own integrity, and doesn't necessarily sit easily with another. In the upcoming projects, our community performance making artists, our gallery co-ordinator and I, as director, would be aware of the artistic interaction, and of the events' impact and timing.

## Collaborating

The centre's two community-arts programs – visual and performing arts – were too new for what we attempted: neither yet had a history of collaboration, although it occurred in later projects.

## Putting symbols together

Care has to be taken in putting symbols together. They're potent conveyors of meaning – different messages for different people. When some people view specific symbols, their individual interpretations of these symbols might be filtered through unconscious psychological baggage, perceived social taboos and a deep sense of religious sacrilege.

## Establishing the task group

We established a gallery task group to be a source of advice and support for the Art & Soul Gallery co-ordinator. The task group comprised several local artists, the church minister and me, as the PCLC's director, and was convened by the gallery co-ordinator. The committee of management formally adopted both the gallery's aims and the selection criteria that were being applied at the time. For the gallery co-ordinator, the task group became a resource for consulting and jointly deciding about whether and when an exhibition would be mounted at the centre. Over the ensuing few years, the group members worked together productively. By forming a task group, I believe we turned a problematic management issue into a positive action.

Managing a community-arts project in a broader organisation is a juggling act at the best of times: you're always checking the various priorities, strategic plans, and program aims and objectives, yet you have to be flexible enough to make changes and adjustments when they're required. A community-service provider is placed at the forefront of defined community needs, and the security of the people who are most vulnerable is one of its moral and legal imperatives.

Another dilemma for arts managers is that of censorship versus artistic freedom, especially in a general-community setting.

Finally, for community-arts management to be successful, it's crucial that all participants be respectful of the various relationships embraced on the host organisation's property and in its programs.

# 9

# Behind the scenes

The management personnel of the host organisation have to establish effective business practices in order both to maintain the organisation's internal projects and to meet public regulations and funding requirements. In this chapter, we use the PCLC experience to set out clear processes and suggestions for managing a community-performance project, from employing the community artist/s to ticking off the items on a project-management checklist. In Chapter 10, we discuss how to manage the project financially. Again, we intend these suggestions to be helpful hints for running projects smoothly – they're not prescriptive for each project.

## Supporting the projects at the PCLC

The PCLC provides the annual Community Performance Making project with continuity, evaluation, reflection and maintenance. Core organisational staff members back up the projects by managing them, doing the administrative work, obtaining funding, preparing submissions for grants, writing acquittal reports, maintaining relations with arts–team members, and undertaking forward planning and community development.

Vanessa Case, one of the two community artists who worked on our 1998 project, *Best Foot Forward*, used her evaluative statement to reflect on this tangible support. She stated that in her experience during the project, the following three aspects of organisational practice worked especially well.

- Having help in preparing grant applications and developing the budget
- Being provided with office and rehearsal space in order to help consolidate the project's existence
- Having access to managers, who were the equivalent of mentors, guides and supporters, when dealing with issues that were more than purely functional

# Managing the Community Performance Making Program

## The project's aims and objectives

The aims of the PCLC's Community Performance Making Program 'feed into' each project and are identified in the position description we give the key artist/s. Each project also has its own specific aims, which are clear and realistic. In formulating the project's objectives, the PCLC's managers take into account the community or participants involved, the project's intention and scope, and the likely outcomes. For examples of the details of the aims and objectives of the three projects we discuss in this book, please read chapters 3, 4 and 5.

For each of the three annual projects we discuss, we drew up the centre's objectives in collaboration with the sponsoring body, the key artist/s and the community, and revisited them periodically during the project. We then developed measurable outcomes for each.

## Critical factors for achieving the objectives

By formulating the project's objectives, we were able to identify the resources that would be required, for example quantitative items such as venues for performance and rehearsal, processes and workshops, and equipment and skills. We were also able to clarify other critical factors that are important for the venture's success, such as planning well, communicating effectively, devising timeframes for developing and delivering the project, formulating the project's guiding principles, and deciding how the project would be evaluated. In identifying these objectives, we were able to set priorities, provide the project with some focus and identify potential problems. We were also able to commence outlining a budget (see Chapter 10).

Other factors had a qualitative aspect, because they were more relational. It was through these factors, however, that social outcomes were achieved for both individuals and the community. In Figure 9.1, on page 116, we include a checklist we've devised to track a project's organisational progress in the Community Performance Making Program.

**Figure 9.1** Checklist: organisational progress.

# Checklist for Managing a Community Performance Making Program[22]

This checklist is a guide for single artists or small arts teams working with a host organisation to manage a community performance making project, and can also be used by the auspicing body.[23]

☐ Aims and objectives stated: the proposed project's intentions, description, scope and outcomes, and collaboration of the sponsoring organisation, arts team and community

☐ Critical factors listed: for successfully achieving the project's outcomes – resources, partnerships, priorities, budget estimates and potential problems

☐ Position description of key artist/s: including the main functions, required skills, responsibilities, remuneration and employment conditions

☐ Sufficient funding: for the project's sponsorship and grant submissions, and in-kind support

☐ Criteria for selecting key artist/s: for example having continuity of a community-arts focus and being a local resident, and eliciting the name/s of the artist/s, for example by advertising the annual position, by inviting a known artist, and by having a local arts officer nominate someone

☐ Advertising position: if included in the selection procedures

☐ Interviewing: of the candidate/s for the position of key artist/s

☐ Employment: of the selected key artist/s, including preparing a written contract, setting the fees and conditions, calculating the on-costs (WorkCover; superannuation, when it applies; and pro rata annual leave), and obtaining the written acceptance of the artist/s

☐ Physical resources: for the key artist/s – the workspace, desk, phone, files, photocopier and computer access, rehearsal space, keys, and public-liability insurance

☐ Administrative support: messages, typing and photocopying, petty cash, and bookkeeping

☐ Project accountability: copyright, financial monitoring, contract of service, health and safety, project-acquittal reports, and auditing

☐ Project Advisory Group (not the same as the arts team): for brainstorming ideas, monitoring the processes, and supporting the key artist/s during the project

☐ Orientation and organisational management of key artist/s: orienting the host organisation's staff members, introducing the community members, monitoring the pace of the key artist/s and health outcomes, and providing support for the arts team

☐ Collection of project documentation: both visual and written documentation

☐ Closure process: completing the rituals of closure – celebrating, giving tangible gifts, handing back the keys and resources, preparing a written reference for the key artist/s or stating your availability for preparing a reference in the future

☐ Regular reporting: to the Project Advisory Group, the director or manager and/or the organisation's board

☐ Project evaluation: evaluation of the project's outcomes

© Preston Creative Living Centre, *Community Performance Making Program Manual*, 1996

Many of the processes we've noted on this project-management checklist are time consuming for a host organisation to complete. At the PCLC, we integrated them in the centre's day-to-day workings. When you're planning your project, you'll have to consider whether you need to build additional administrative or managerial support into the project budget.

Another critical factor to consider is whether to form one or more strategic partnerships for the project and how to successfully negotiate these preferred partnerships, from beginning to end. The type of partnership can vary: it can be a formalised partnership, a natural alliance, or an informal contribution.

## Formalised partnerships

At the PCLC, we developed a formalised partnership by making a contractual arrangement with, for example, the City of Darebin – our municipal council – and the Diana Ferrari Shoe Factory. The City of Darebin partnership was essential for the success we enjoyed in each project. Although, on an operational basis, the contact we had was with the council's Arts and Cultural Planner, the link itself was contractually with the actual local-government authority. We found it both necessary and relevant to forge this link in order to mount strong and effective projects. Local government was necessarily the appropriate layer of government for obtaining helpful resources and referrals. Local government was most relevant for us in mounting our community projects, because we were also relying on the goodwill of the community's formal aspects, of which the City of Darebin was an obvious expression.

## Natural alliances

When partners form a natural alliance, they share basic interests and agendas. Potential partners include the health and welfare sector, community education, schools and universities, community-arts networks, organised-art groups, and municipal councils. For the PCLC, an example of a natural alliance was the birth educator's association with *Once Upon Your Birthday*.

## Informal contributions

Informal contributors can 'walk in your door' at any time, having heard about your project. In our *Spinning, Weaving* project, for example, community member Harold Osborne became an active participant when he came to the centre to repair a loom and decided to stay. He wove part of the five-panel woollen backdrop, participated in a storytelling workshop, and became one of the final performance's ten key spinners.

## The position description

One of the requirements of employing people to work on a project is to have a well-written position description, in this case for the project's key artist/s. In some management processes, the document has to be cleared by either a personnel task group or a board of governance before selection procedures, such as advertising the position, can be put in place. For some funding submissions, it might be necessary to have a position description as part of the detail of the submission, as in the case of submissions addressed to the Australia Council for the Arts.

**Figure 9.2** The position description.

---

# Position Description

**Position:**        Community Artist (Performing Arts)

**Key functions:**   To work with the Darebin community, especially the members of the Preston–Reservoir community, to encourage local residents in developing community arts – performing, theatrical, musical and visual – and provide a high-quality arts experience as the culmination of the project

To extend the learning of the selected artist/s in his/her/their art medium, for example choreography, vocals, design or storytelling, by way of the project's workshopping and performance event

---

**Skills required:**

1. Community recognition as a quality artist in his/her/their medium/media
2. Proven ability to mount a community performance through a model for developing community arts
3. Cross-cultural experience
4. Management of a small arts team
5. Facilitation of special-interest workshops
6. Professional development of local artists
7. Networking skills within community groups and arts organisations
8. Empathy with the PCLC's vision

The artist is expected to be a resident of the City of Darebin or its immediate environs.

**Responsibilities:**

1. To provide an innovative and inclusive Darebin-community event within the year of the project
2. To foster the community artists' network associated with the PCLC

3. To create a supportive environment in which community members can participate in creating an arts performance
4. To workshop around the theme agreed on for the project, in terms of both images and performance
5. To produce the performance within the project's budgetary constraints, for example with reference to grants obtained and other available funds
6. To prepare publicity and promotional materials and documentation of the project year

**Remuneration:**

As per the appropriate award

**Conditions:**

WorkCover, superannuation and annual leave provided as per the award

Reimbursement of project expenses within the budget

Office space and a phone made available at the PCLC; fax and photocopier access made available

Administrative support, including bookkeeping, provided

---

In Figure 9.2, opposite, we include an edited version of the position description we devised in 1996 for selecting our key artist/s. It contains the main elements that survived the three projects we discuss in the book.

A position description is important as a document that's been agreed on by the employed artist and the host organisation. It's useful for clarifying both the artist's role and the employer's expectations. Also, at the end of the employment period, you'll benefit by using it as a tool for preparing a professional evaluation and securing closure.

During our three projects, the PCLC also met other basic employment standards, in accordance with the federal *Workplace Relations Act* 1996, as well as with industry awards such as the Entertainment and Broadcasting Industry (Actors [Theatrical]) Award 1998 and the Media, Entertainment and Arts Alliance Award. We discuss these requirements in more detail in the sections headed 'On-costs', on page 122, and 'Project accountability', under 'Copyright', on page 124.

## Funding

We discuss the process of fundraising for a community-arts project in Chapter 10. Suffice it to say that you have to have sufficient funding before you can employ an artist or proceed with the project.

Part of the early funding activity for any project is to identify the resources you require for the project and to enter the items, such as fees for the artist/s, direct project costs, and administrative support, in your budget estimates.

## Selection criteria

Once an organisation has successfully secured the funding, the designated person approaches the desired artist/s and presents a concrete offer to employ him/her/them within a given year or period of a project.

During the PCLC's early years, we had an informal selection process. However, as the Community Performance Making Program continues, the PCLC is finding that it's becoming necessary to have more-formal procedures.

During the earlier years, one of the key criteria for each selection was to clearly stipulate that the community artist/s resided in Darebin. In including this qualification, the PCLC executive hoped that the artist/s would bring to the project some knowledge and appreciation of the area, that encouragement would be there for people to form local networks of interested individuals and participants by way of the key artist's contacts, and that long-term benefits would ensue for a healthy arts practice in the area.

## Advertising

You might find it easy to locate an experienced artist by making use of the host organisation's established connections. If you don't, you'll find it useful to advertise.

When you advertise in order to find a local artist, consider using local-media resources: community radio, local print media – newspapers and community print news, local-government links, and informal networks of artists. It's also appropriate to advertise via community-arts networks and, budget permitting, the major newspapers' employment section.

In the state of Victoria, the Arts Access organisation provides a free-access Internet database of community artists, and Australia's other states and territories might have a similar online resource.

## Interviewing the artist candidate/s

When you come to interview the artists you've short-listed, you need to do two things: allow adequate time for a constructive conversation, and organise a small panel of people who have appropriate skills and associations. For example, four member categories you might consider for your interviewing panel are a representative of the sponsoring or auspicing organisation, a person who has artistic experience in the performing arts, a person who's experienced in community development and a person who has knowledge of the local area.

It's helpful if the members of the interviewing panel have agreed on the set of questions through which they'll obtain the necessary information from each candidate on a consistent basis.

## Employing the selected artist

It's essential to offer the selected artist a contract of employment, which includes the agreed-on salary or artist's fees, the length of the employment period, and the terms and conditions. For a small fee, the Arts Law Centre of Australia provides sample contracts both for employing artists-in-residence and for employing artists in a community context.[25]

## Salary and fees[26]

Setting the fees you're to pay the artist/s is a necessary adjunct to preparing the job description. The actual salary or artist fees you finally offer can vary according to the length of the artist's experience and the timeframe of his or her employment. However, it's essential you decide on a range of fees that's realistic in terms of both the project's funding and the desired outcome, and, at the same time, that in deciding the fees you treat the artist/s equitably.

In Australia, depending on whether the artist has an Australian Business Number (ABN), you might have to pay him or her under the category of staff member rather than contractor.

Several industrial awards and fee structures are available for you to consider. You can contact the relevant body, such as the Media, Entertainment and Arts Alliance (MEAA) or the Musicians' Union, which are the relevant unions for performing artists. Another good resource for deciding on payment rates for community performing artists who are to work in community cultural development projects is the Queensland Community Arts Network. Peak bodies can provide practical advice, especially when the community performing arts project covers a number of tasks, as opposed to clearly regulated roles as set out in some state or federal awards.

The two parties – the host organisation and the artist – have to agree on the payment schedule, and the schedule has to be relevant to the work patterns required for the project. For the three projects that the PCLC undertook between 1995 and 1999, we provided part-time wages and conditions until the final weeks, during which the artist/s ran rehearsals and staged the performance. In these culminating activities, the producer – who was also the key artist – and the other core artists were required to be committed to the project on a full-time basis. The director and the artist agreed on these arrangements beforehand, and a written copy of these agreed hours was attached to the signed contract.

According to the remuneration method that the PCLC's managers used, the key artists were paid on a fortnightly basis, after the artist presented a timesheet. This timesheet was counter-signed, in turn, by the director, and was presented to the accountant. During the key artist's fortnight, the agreed hours fluctuated according to the number and nature of the workshops and performance periods.

## On-costs

On-costs are employee-related costs that the host organisation incurs over and above the direct-salary costs. In Australia, these costs are usually associated with payments for WorkCover, which is compulsory employee insurance; payments for superannuation, which is a federally mandated employer contribution to employees' retirement funds; and an allocated payment for annual leave.

### WorkCover

WorkCover[27] is calculated at a percentage of gross wages; in 2001, the PCLC expended 2.5 per cent of wages on the allowance. In accordance with the federal government's existing Superannuation Guarantee policies, you pay superannuation at 8 per cent of gross wages if the artist's earning capacity surpasses the monthly threshold amount of $450 (the 2001 rate). At the PCLC, annual leave is calculated at four weeks per year, or on a *pro rata* basis if the employee isn't working at the centre full time. The accountant calculates annual leave at one-twelfth of the total basic salary the employee receives each year, and pays it along with a 17.5 per cent leave loading. During the artist's contracted term of employment, he or she can also incur penalty rates, meal allowances and travel costs.[28]

The PCLC used a rough calculation of on-costs as being at 20 per cent of the project's gross wages in order to enable the budget to be planned when we were preparing the early submissions and to recover the organisational costs.

## Physical resources, including public liability

The PCLC provided the key artist and the program participants with both office space and rehearsal space. The artist was given access to a computer, a photocopier, a sound system, and keys for using the premises after business hours.

The administrative-staff members made rehearsal space available on a 'booking' basis, and gave priority to the PCLC's programs. When you make rehearsal and performance spaces available, you have to meet statutory requirements for insurance coverage.

At the PCLC, we covered our paid staff members by providing WorkCover insurance against any injury or disability that occurred during their specified employment at the centre. As the host organisation undertaking a project, you'll also have to insure your performing-arts staff members under WorkCover or a similar scheme that operates in your country.

You should secure Public Liability Insurance for all other activities covered in the project, and Volunteer Workers Insurance for volunteers who are contributing to the host organisation or its project. To ensure that your performers, artists, production personnel and volunteers are covered when they're performing in venues other than your own base – in our case the PCLC – you should also arrange policy coverage.

You should seek insurance quotations in writing, and in order to select the best broker or company, we advise you to describe the project's activities in full detail. In determining your insurance coverage, you might find your municipal council or sponsoring organisation helpful. You might fall under its policy as being a recognised program or under emerging community-liability schemes being established. Unfortunately, the premiums are rising, so you have to be realistic in your budgeting.

## Administrative support

In the PCLC's three projects, the administrative officers provided back-up support in the form of taking phone messages, typing, photocopying, welcoming the participants, and selling tickets and 'working the doors' before the performances. They also reconciled the petty cash and, together with the accountant, paid the project accounts. An independent artist working within your organisation will find it invaluable to have strong administrative support.

> The centre and the program provided the base for these experiences to take shape, through administration, through workshops and through liaison with industries, with good working relationships with the staff and community participants.
> – 1998–99 production director Christos Linou

## Project accountability

The key artist and host organisation should clarify the procedures for accountability when the artist commences employment. For some areas of accountability, responsibility clearly lies with the artist; for others, it lies with the auspicing body or employer, and for yet others, it's shared. The key areas of accountability are monitoring the finances; delivering the project within an agreed timeframe and to an agreed standard; monitoring who owns copyright; meeting health and safety obligations; meeting the legal requirements to do with, for example, equal opportunity and WorkCover; and working to the employer's contract of service.

### Copyright

At this point in the book, we note several points about copyright, because at the time of writing, it was an issue that people in the field were discussing at length. Copyright is a set of legal rights through which ownership of creative works is specified. Copyright owners have the right to determine what people can or can't do with the work, for example reproduce it in another context, film it or publish it. The copyright owner also has the right to benefit financially from the work.

Because community-performance projects usually involve active participation of community members in creating the work, negotiating copyright can be a complex task. Project managers also have to consider moral rights. Moral rights are the personal rights of creators of artwork to, for example, publicly claim authorship of the work.

You can't ignore copyright issues: you have to deal with them early in the project's life. However, you needn't be daunted by the process: useful resources are available to help you negotiate it.[29]

According to the current wisdom in the community-arts field, project managers have to consider copyright issues carefully during the project's early stages and negotiate contracts in which they honour all the partners' rights. In negotiating a contract, therefore, you also have to envisage under what future circumstances someone might use the work; enter into an agreement about the work's ownership; and ensure that the agreement is, as much as possible, as equitable and fair as possible for all the parties involved. When you're framing the agreement, you have to take into consideration your project's specific features.

If the parties don't negotiate a contract, all the *Copyright Act* regulations come into play, and these can be difficult and complex to apply in community-arts contexts.[30]

## The *Privacy Act*

Another legal requirement that might impact on project accountability is the *Privacy Act*, in the form of federal or state legislation such as the Victorian act, which applies from 1 September 2002.[31] Although usual personnel procedures apply to personal information about paid and volunteer artists, collection of personal information about community participants during workshops can vary. When you're circulating a contact sheet in, for example, a storytelling or dance workshop, it's advisable to have written on the top of the sheet:

- Personal and contact details are *optional*.
- The purpose of this workshop is . . .

It's expected that the facilitating artists will treat this information respectfully and carefully. If you wish to print personal stories that emerge from the community-arts project, written permission forms are necessary; otherwise, names and identifiers are avoided. Sponsoring bodies are already bound by the *Privacy Act*.

## The Project Advisory Group

The PCLC's managers established and convened an advisory group for each of the three projects. Each group included the key artist, the PCLC director and one outside person who had desired skills, in an area such as public relations or arts management; all three parties attended the meetings on a voluntary basis. During the meetings, the key artist was able to brainstorm ideas and processes within a group that comprised people who were committed to community arts as well as people who were removed from the project's day-to-day activities and decision making. In Table 9.1, we list the members of the Project Advisory Group formed for each project.

**Table 9.1** The members of the project advisory groups

| Once Upon Your Birthday | Spinning, Weaving: Trees and Songs | Best Foot Forward |
|---|---|---|
| Beth Shelton, project director | Bagryana Popov, project director | Vanessa Case, key co-artist |
| | | Christos Linou, production director |
| Judi Fisher, PCLC director | Judi Fisher, PCLC director | |
| Jenni Stokes, community-development consultant | Alice Nash, production director | Judi Fisher, PCLC director |
| | | Barbara Doherty, Arts Access representative |

## Orientation and organisational management of the artist

The PCLC aimed to have a creative and constructive working relationship between the key artist and the centre manager. We nurtured the relationship in several specific ways. The artist was able to directly contact Judi, as the director, in order to find out information and report on how the project was progressing. In the project's early stages, this factor was critical for the artist to be able to absorb the PCLC's ethos and monitor the project's development in line with the agreed-on concepts of the Community Performance Making Program. It's important that the artist feel part of the organisation.

# Reporting regularly

By having an agreed-on and set routine for the key artist/s to report on the project's progress, we were able to both confirm this progress and alleviate any emerging problems. When project managers use the reporting well, it becomes an engaging and creative process.

At the PCLC, the key artist reported regularly via the Project Advisory Group and regularly had appointments with the centre manager in order to provide project updates. During these conversations, the artist and manager checked the project for how it was developing conceptually, discussed the results of the workshop, kept track of the project-delivery dates, monitored the resources and finances, prepared the performance, and allowed for adjustments as required.

# Evaluating the project

The PCLC has standard personnel routines for its staff members, including the annual staff-performance assessment. During our three projects, we gave the key artist/s access to the following three routines that are part of the assessment.

1. Evaluation of the past year, in line with both the duties stated in the position description and initiatives taken during the year
2. Planning for learning opportunities for the staff member to take up over the ensuing year
3. Co-ordinating the requirements of the centre's programs

For the key artists, with whom the PCLC had a limited arrangement, the assessment was an opportunity for them to focus on evaluating their own performance and goal achievements. The manager also built two other aspects into the assessment: the opportunity for the artists to report to the PCLC board on the project's final results, and the opportunity for the PCLC to affirm the artist's future professional hopes and to offer job references later on.

# Collecting documentation

Documentation is the record of the project: material, visual and recorded. In any project, you need to incorporate collecting and preserving the documentation from the beginning, so negotiation between the key artist/s and host organisation has to occur early on. For all three PCLC projects, the artist/s kept various types of journal in order to record how the project was developing, both conceptually and performance wise. The PCLC has archived these journals, as well as photos; film; videotapes, and a complete set of posters, flyers and programs.

Two things we at the PCLC learned during this experience are that you have to:

1. credit the photographer/s, designer/s and artist/s who worked on each project and to retain the information about the credits with the archival material
2. retain a full list of the project participants so you can contact them later to discuss other projects if necessary.

## Undertaking the process for closure
### Partying and gift giving

Closure was important in each of these projects. For the performance participants, the PCLC and the arts team organised parties and devised cleaning-up routines so the participants could celebrate, we could thank and affirm each of them, and we and they might exchange contact details. On the final-performance night or at the final farewell, a delegated PCLC member gave the key artist/s a tangible gift, as an expression of appreciation for a task well done, and as a token of esteem and remembrance.

### Writing the acquittal report

In each of the three projects, the key artist's final tasks included writing the acquittal report. Funding bodies usually have their own acquittal-report forms for the artist to complete. The forms vary for artists and host organisations, but you'll find them to be useful guides for accountability.

If you have other details that are important to convey to the funding body, the form will usually include an 'Other' heading under which you can add the information; otherwise, you can simply attach your comments to the form. Many funding bodies also request some type of visual information about the project. In

PHOTO: JUDI FISHER

**Figure 9.3** Along with the applause come the celebrating and evaluating: some of the *Best Foot Forward* cast members celebrating the December 1998 final performance.

our reports, we tried to include several colour photos – usually colour photocopies – because in them, we'd graphically captured the project's essence. In some cases, the funding body later requested permission to use the visuals.

It's critical that you submit the acquittal report in order to mark the project's completion and that you do so within the funding body's allocated timeframe.

You might also wish to lodge a copy of the report with Queensland's Performing Arts Museum or the Community Arts Resource Collection (CARC), which is a national collection for documenting community-arts projects and processes.[32]

## Conversing and actively observing

At the PCLC, the key artist/s had a closing conversation with the director. During the meeting:

- the director collected the various keys the artist/s had been using
- the director and artist/s completed and signed off on the final timesheet/s so that the artist/s could receive the final payment/s
- the director and artist/s reached an understanding about

providing other professional references

- the PCLC's staff members informally expressed their
appreciation to the artist/s, sometimes in an afternoon-tea
setting.

Over the years, the PCLC's director, staff members and board
members have found it rewarding to actively observe how a
former key artist's career is developing and to attend other project
performances, exhibitions or events in which the artist features.
Similarly, former community participants find it heart warming to
revisit the PCLC, or to meet a staff member in the street, and
share a greeting and news.

### 'Captured moments': a reflection from Judi

*I was there each year, watching the energy and images
emerging daily. I observed the artists skilfully eliciting the
community members' stories. I experienced the fever pitch of
rehearsals and performances during which both the participants
and the audience members were moved and delighted.*

*I remember captured moments during which people were
transformed, moments in which exquisite theatre, emotive
dance and heart-stopping revelations were offered through
community performance. The participants' stories and songs
were incredibly generous, poignant, rich and rare gifts.*

*These gifts came from 'ordinary' people, both long-term
residents and more-recent arrivals, living in our streets and
neighbourhoods – Maria, Cliff, Jo, Rhea and Mukles.
However, in terms of both their courage and their contribution,
they revealed themselves to be extraordinary.*

*We were no longer strangers. We understood each other
better, and many of us became friends in the process.*

## A summary of our three projects

In Table 9.2, opposite and on page 132, we summarise various
aspects of our three projects, including management, funding
sources and budgets, roles, and timeframes. We hope you're able to
use the information to compare the projects' individual
components.

**Table 9.2** The summary

| Component | *Once Upon Your Birthday* | *Spinning, Weaving: Trees and Songs* | *Best Foot Forward* |
|---|---|---|---|
| Project description | A multi-arts project in which the focus was on dance; a site-specific performance and community celebration at the PCLC | A multi-arts project in which the focus was on family stories; a site-specific performance on two nights at the PCLC | A multi-arts project over an extended timeframe, in which the focus was on feet, shoes and Darebin's shoe industry; four major site-specific performances and six visual exhibitions over eighteen months |
| Community | A geographical community: the Preston–Reservoir neighbourhood<br><br>Multi-age<br><br>A community of interest in birth<br><br>Culturally diverse; for example strong Ghanaian and Pontian-Greek representation<br><br>The local-parish community of the Preston Uniting Church | Multi-age<br><br>A geographical community: the city of Darebin<br><br>A community of interest in storytelling, spinning or weaving<br><br>Culturally diverse: Iraqi, Indonesian, Bulgarian, Serbian, Canadian, United States, English and Irish representation<br><br>The local-parish community | Multi-age<br><br>A geographical community: the city of Darebin<br><br>A community of interest in dance and movement<br><br>Culturally diverse<br><br>The shoe industry, including the Diana Ferrari Shoe Factory<br><br>Several local primary schools: selected Grade 1 and Grade 6 students<br><br>People who had a disability |
| Purpose and aims | To initiate a quality community creative process and performance in Preston–Reservoir<br><br>To re-frame and artistically celebrate the body and movement in birth<br><br>To contribute to development of local community arts practice<br><br>To increase community awareness of the PCLC as being a local resource and art space<br><br>To create an event through which cultural diversity would be promoted and cross-cultural networks would be created | To provide a performance for the Darebin community on two nights<br><br>To workshop around life stories and songs, both inherited and local<br><br>To create a singular, innovative and inclusive piece of music and theatre performance of significant quality for the Darebin community's enjoyment | To provide a cultural celebration of feet, shoes and dancing<br><br>To suggest the diversity of Darebin's cultural community in work, dance and recreation<br><br>To skill the artists to include, in movement workshops, people who had a disability<br><br>To establish a series of events in which the area's shoe history would be incorporated<br><br>To enter into a community-arts partnership with a local shoe factory<br><br>To present a quality, multimedia performance in the shoe factory |

**Table 9.2** The summary (continued)

| Component | *Once Upon Your Birthday* | *Spinning, Weaving: Trees and Songs* | *Best Foot Forward* |
|---|---|---|---|
| Project team | Beth Shelton, choreographer and key artist; Julie Perrin, storyteller co ordinator; Mahoney Kiely, directorial assistant, and visual and fire artist; Clare de Bruin, drummer and community drum co-ordinator; Bagryana Popov, Petrunka-choir musical director; Stephanie Francis, publicist | Bagryana Popov, theatre creator; Ilka White, project and set designer; Alice Nash, project assistant; the Petrunka choir, musical backing; Deborah Hatton, publicist and production co-ordinator | Vanessa Case, choreographer and key artist; Christos Linou, production director and dancer; Marina Bistrin, dancer; Liz Landray, music producer; Monica Tessalaar, publicist |
| Project timeframe | 21 weeks; Beth: 59 days | 26 weeks; Bagryana: 67 days 4 weeks; re-mount: 20 days | Christos: 18 months, mostly part time; Vanessa: 12 months |
| 'Effective full time' hours of key artist/s | 413 hours, or 11.8 weeks | 469 hours, or 13.4 weeks | Multiple activities – over eighteen months; not comparable |
| Management | Managed by the PCLC and a project steering committee Administered jointly by Judi Fisher and Beth Shelton Accountable to the PCLC treasurer and executive committee | Managed by the PCLC and a project steering committee Administered by Judi Fisher Accountable to the PCLC treasurer and executive committee | Managed by the PCLC and a project steering committee Administered by Judi Fisher Accountable to the PCLC treasurer and executive committee |
| Funding sources | The Australia Council for the Arts (a federal body) Arts Victoria (a state body) Darebin City Council (the municipal council) | The Australia Council for the Arts (a federal body) Darebin City Council (the municipal council) Darebin City Council (for the re-mount) The Preston Uniting Church Parish | The Australia Council for the Arts (a federal body) Darebin City Council (the municipal council) The Diana Ferrari Shoe Factory |
| In-kind support | The PCLC | The PCLC The re-mount: La Mama Theatre, the PCLC, and cast members and ther friends and relatives | The PCLC The Diana Ferrari Shoe Factory |
| Budget | $27,500 | $24,000 | $38,000 |
| Income | $27,476 | $23,153 Re-mount: $3000 | $38,346 |
| Expenses | $27,476 | $23,156 Re-mount: $3000 | $38,298 |

# 10 Breaking even – or better!

A successfully funded project requires a good idea, some key people with experience to enable the project to be achieved, and an agency with a reputation for reliability. – **City of Darebin Senior Arts and Cultural Planner Mark Wilkinson**

Although these three factors are essential for a project to attract funding, securing the funds is only one aspect of a community-arts project's financial management. In this chapter, we anticipate some of the key issues that arise and that we had to address. In Figure 10.1, on page 134, we provide a checklist of key components commonly encountered in financial management of a community-arts project.

We devote most of the chapter to outlining some of the stages that can be involved in the financial management, from conceiving the project to preparing the annual report and audited financial statements. Again, these stages are not definitive: we intend them to be guiding steps within the project. The stages are:

- conceiving the project
- preparing the proposed budget
- researching the designated funds and appropriate sources of moneys
- obtaining the grant-application forms and relevant information
- applying for an administered grant through an auspicing body if the artist is initiating the project
- obtaining clarification or advice from selected fund managers
- writing the grant submission
- obtaining letters of support
- establishing clear financial-accountability processes
- obtaining in-kind support
- redrafting the budget
- establishing lines of financial accounting
- preparing financial statements on a regular basis
- evaluating the project
- writing the acquittal report
- auditing the financial accounts
- preparing the annual report and audited financial statements.

We conclude the chapter by discussing the external factors involved in forward planning your community performance making program.

# Checklist for Financially Managing the Project[33]

This checklist is a guide for host organisations to use in financially managing the community performance-making process.

- [ ] Project conception
- [ ] Proposed budget for project: for example the anticipated and realistic costings for the conceptual stage, the developmental stage and the performance stage
- [ ] Research of designated funds and appropriate sources of moneys
- [ ] Obtaining grant-application forms and relevant information: for example policies, criteria and funding limits
- [ ] Administered grant with auspicing body (if artist initiated): for example are incorporated, have an Australian Business Number, have a good community and/or artistic reputation, and have a business partnership
- [ ] Clarification or advice from selected fund managers in submitting to their funding bodies
- [ ] Written grant submission
- [ ] Obtained letters of support for funding applications
- [ ] Clear financial-accountability processes within the auspicing body
- [ ] In-kind support: through partnerships and/or sponsors, or by the auspicing body
- [ ] Redraft of budget when the funding has been acquired
- [ ] Lines of financial accounting: petty cash, bookkeeping, and payment of accounts and fees
- [ ] Regular financial statements against budget, to evaluate costs against income projections
- [ ] Evaluation of the project in line with the budget, income and expenditure
- [ ] Acquittal report: not necessary to have the financial statement audited at this stage
- [ ] Audit
- [ ] Auspicing body's annual reports and audited financial statements

**Figure 10.1** Checklist: financial management of the project.

© Preston Creative Living Centre, *Community Performance Making Program Manual*, 1996.

# Conceiving the project

Every project requires a funding strategy, and funding is a double bind: you can't employ an artist until after you've secured the funding, and you can't secure the funding without having devised a viable and detailed artistic concept and plan.

When you're formulating strategies and preparing submissions for your project, it's often difficult to balance the gains and losses – it's a bit like playing a game of Snakes and Ladders, because the successful mix is the result of many factors. The PCLC's main strategic resolution during this period was to apply for funding for two stages of each project; that is, funding for each stage would come from a different source. The two stages were:

- the conceptual and research stage
- the performance-making stage.

The PCLC sought funding for the conceptual and research stage from the municipal council, the City of Darebin. Using this smaller grant, the key artists were able to start shaping their project, to conceive the project's theme, to undertake the early workshopping of the theme, and to gather together potential participants and other artists.

While this first stage was in process and the theme was taking shape, we sought funding for the performance-making stage, from, for example, the Australia Council for the Arts or another arts body. A measure of risk was always involved in terms of eventually achieving the full project. The key artist's conceptual input was valuable for the project's artistic drive, however, and through the workshopping, community input was introduced in the performance's shaping and content.[34]

At the PCLC, management of a realistic timeframe for submission of grant applications is required in order to support continuity of the Community Performance Making Program. As we've stated, a measure of risk is involved in this management area: financial risk, for the host organisation, that 'underwrites' the time the managers require in order to develop the proposals and write the submissions, and personal and professional risk, for the artist, who, if the application is unsuccessful, might be employed at the conceptual stage but not funded through to the performance-making stage.

## Preparing the proposed budget

When you're preparing the project-funding submission, you have to prepare a budget. When you submit the funding request, the budget has to be as close as possible to a realistic and costed 'guesstimate'. You can determine the cost of items such as artists' fees by checking award rates, but you can estimate the costs of the costumes and performance only by basing the estimate on other, similar experiences. In Australia, you also have to 'factor in' GST – the Goods and Services Tax.[35]

In Figure 10.3, on page 145, we include the budget from our second project, *Spinning, Weaving: Trees and Songs*. Note the four key components: direct production income; wages, salaries and fees; administration costs; and documentation. Some funding bodies have their own financial categories for budgeting, and you have to use these categories when you're preparing your submission. Some funding bodies stipulate that you designate, in a separate column, the components of the budget for which you're asking them to provide moneys.

## Researching the designated funds and appropriate sources of moneys

Writing grant applications is an essential part of the processes involved in community-arts projects – although many beginning artists might feel like our key artists did!

In Australia, funding programs are usually in place at all three levels of government: federal, state and local. A myriad of government-funded agencies also exist that disburse significant funds. Private institutions, especially philanthropic trusts, can also be a significant source of funding.

In the community, there are also people, such as local-government cultural planners, who know about the processes involved in applying for funds, are aware of the structure, and can help artists. Many experienced community artists will happily tell you who, in their local scene, gave them a helping hand.

For most people and many artists, funding is opaque.
– Alice

It's the invisible stuff.
– Bagryana

Intimidating.
– Beth

# Obtaining the grant-application forms and relevant information

When you're preparing your grant application, you have to take into consideration the central policies that 'drive' each funding agency, as well as the trends that are emerging within specific types of grant.

Most funding bodies have written criteria that you can request by phone, in writing or online. Their material can also include set application forms.

Some funding sources, such as the Australia Council for the Arts, have highly specific criteria for making their funding selections. OzCouncil, for example, has inclusiveness policies in which it requires specific information about your project's mix of gender, age, ethnicity, locality and skills.

Trust funds have clear objectives and preferred areas of philanthropic interest. It's therefore important that you obtain accurate information and are selective.[36] Read their information carefully, and select funding sources that are appropriate for your project: when you're applying for community-arts funding, there's no point in applying to a trust that has a main interest in medical research!

If you're either an artist or a program manager, it's also advisable to attend designated funding bodies' information-and-advice seminars when they're advertised. Two examples are the seminars that many municipal councils hold, and the advertised annual seminars that the Australia Council for the Arts holds in regional areas when it releases its policies and annual handbook.

When a project is being delivered, a professional working relationship develops between the project, the host organisation and the funding body. This is the point at which reputations are created, and a community-arts program becomes known within performing-arts circles and among the funding bodies.

At the PCLC, when we were applying for grants, everyone involved – the director, the executive board members and the project artists – tried to maintain integrity according to the centre's own values and principles, and to then determine where the funding body's policies and our principles meshed. These points became crucial each year when we were writing the submissions. For example, we were working in a community that included many senior citizens, so when the City of Darebin was giving weight to community groups that were working with it during the Year of the Older Person, the PCLC had already established the priority of including older community members.

With reference to amounts of funds available to community groups and arts organisations, there are sometimes stated limitations. For example, in our case, because the City of Darebin was trying to promote a wide variety of projects and encourage a wide range of groups to participate, it was making smaller grants available. Over time, the PCLC's managers conceived the idea of applying to the council for a small grant in order to pay for the conceptual-workshop stages of each artist's residency, and of reserving our larger-funding application to the federal Community Cultural Development Fund, an arm of the Australia Council for the Arts, for the performance-making stages.

## Applying for an administered grant through an auspicing body if the artist is initiating the project

Many funding bodies stipulate that an incorporated body – a legally recognised entity – administer the grant. It's often the case that for the project to be considered eligible for grant submissions, the artist needs to be auspiced by a third party – an organisation that either has this 'incorporated' status or is a company limited by guarantee. The auspicing body then counter-signs and administers any funding agreement – usually in instalments – for the grant recipient. It's not uncommon for the auspicing body to ask for an auspicing fee in exchange for administering the grant on the artist's behalf. An example of a commonly charged fee is 3 per cent of the total project budget; however, the fee is highly variable as well as negotiable.

It's important that the artist and the auspicing body be clear about their roles, investment and involvement. This understanding is often defined in a written agreement that applies for the project's life. Although it's the auspicing body's responsibility to inform the funding source of any changes that are being proposed for the project – in how the funds are to be used, or with reference to major budgetary alterations or a change of key personnel – the main relationship is between the funding source and the grant recipient.

To receive grants, not-for-profit organisations have to have ABN (Australian Business Number) status and an ABN itself, and can register with the Australian Taxation Office as a Gift Recipient organisation in order to receive project donations.

## Obtaining clarification or advice from selected fund managers

It's possible, and in some cases advisable, to contact selected fund managers in order to clarify details and 'run your request past them' for advice. It's our experience that fund managers are very generous in giving their advice when you have genuine questions to ask and a well thought-out project plan to discuss. Some fund managers helpfully referred us at the PCLC to other funds and trusts when it was clear that either their own funds were limited or our community-arts project was more likely to appeal to another funding body.

We also found that it didn't 'hurt our cause' to phone within a week after the submission deadline in order to check that the funding body had received our submission. In one instance, the PCLC director discovered that an application had been lost in the mail; however, she'd recorded the Express Post satchel number, so she was able to persuade the fund manager to accept the application in the subsequent round of submissions. As a result of that successful negotiation, the PCLC submission was kept alive, and all the hours of work put into 'detailing' it weren't in vain.

## Writing the grant submission

When you're writing the submissions for the grant funding, you're selling your ideas for an opportunity to achieve a successful outcome. To sell your ideas, you have to match your project's aims and objectives with the funding source's criteria, and you have to do so within the funding source's limits, or consider preparing multiple funding applications for a single project.

As we've stated, many funding bodies now include their application form online. Completing the online version of the form is more convenient, because you're not attempting to write within defined and allocated spaces. Also, when you've completed the application, you're better able to send it immediately, although you might be limited in your ability to append attachments in which you illustrate your competence and experience.

For each type of application, you have to plan ahead so you have adequate time to meet the closing dates, seek letters of support, and include visual and/or other material as illustrations of your work. *Know for certain that something unexpected will happen and that you can end up sending the submission in an Express Post satchel on the last possible day!*

Provide all the details about the project clearly and concisely. Convey your ideas imaginatively, energetically and enthusiastically. Indicate:

- who's to be involved, if you already know
- what the project outline is to be
- how the project is to be managed
- how the finances are to be monitored
- what timeframe is to be expected
- what other sources of support are available.

For submissions, longer-term planning and projections towards funding an anticipated project are required. When you're involved in a community performing arts project, it's often the case that you have to rely on downsizing the project 'dream' to fit the resources that become available.

Finally, we advise you to always make photocopies of any submission documents for your files, so you can answer any questions the funding body might have and so you have a resource for any future employed artists to refer to. If you're successful in obtaining the funding, the submission becomes the basis of the contractual arrangements you make with the funding body.

# Obtaining letters of support

Letters of support are letters that collaborating individuals and organisations write in which they express their interest in, enthusiasm for, support for and/or intended participation in your proposed project. Funding bodies often give these letters much weight when they're assessing funding submissions, even though the bodies don't always state that you're required to include the letter/s in your funding application. If you have any doubts about including letters of support, check with the relevant body.

Mark Wilkinson, the City of Darebin's Senior Arts and Cultural Planner,[37] has attended a number of the PCLC's opening nights and exhibitions, and has written several letters of support for its arts-project submissions. In one of the letters, he made the following comments.

> The City of Darebin has supported an annual artist-in-residence program at the Preston Creative Living Centre since 1995. We have done so because we believe that the benefits to the community, both short and long term, have been significant. We also believe that the model developed by the Centre is highly practical and relevant to other community groups, and we encourage other groups to see just how the PCLC does it.
>
> The participants in their projects are local residents who engage in workshopping and performance of community-theatre pieces. The judicious employment of a skilled professional director, such as Bagryana Popov, for the project **Spinning, Weaving: Trees and Songs**, means they are able to support the community participants in a concrete and meaningful way.

# Establishing clear financial-accountability processes

How you intend to manage the funds is critical. The funding body awards the grant to an applicant in the expectation that:

- the applicant will use the funds as indicated
- the organisation that auspices the project will bear financial

responsibility for using the funds appropriately

- in using the funds, the host organisation will establish clear monetary processes and maintain comprehensive financial records, by using a bookkeeper, an accountant or an auditor.

The organisation is to follow these agreed processes in order to fully expend and account for the funds.

If you make *significant* changes to the project budget, you might have to notify the funding body. However, the funding body usually acknowledges that the estimated budget you've presented as part of your funding application won't exactly mirror your project income and expenditure!

## Obtaining in-kind support

In-kind support is non-monetary support for a project. It can originate in the host organisation or among the project's collaborators. It can include items such as raw materials, marketing support, advisory help and venue provision.

In the PCLC's three projects, the organisation found in-kind support to be essential. It generated it in the form of administrative support, office space, phone use, stationery and loss of any rental income on required rehearsal space, along with other incidentals we used in each project.

For the application to proceed with any favour, some funding bodies require the sponsoring body to provide in-kind support. In your submission, it's important you clarify the matter with the specific funding organisation.

From experience, we acknowledge that it's often very difficult for a small organisation to underwrite these facilities on an ongoing basis. At the PCLC, the managers had to look carefully at each project in order to determine what in-kind aspects they could offer. People who are unaccustomed to preparing arts-funding applications sometimes find themselves confused when they're asked to include in-kind contributions within the proposed budget. In order to help you do so, we include the checklist in Figure 10.2, on page 143.

In our third project, *Best Foot Forward*, for example, the Diana Ferrari Shoe Factory, as our project partner, undertook several in-kind aspects of the project (see Chapter 5).

# Checklist for obtaining in-kind support

1. Consider all the items within your project budget that you'd usually have to pay for but that, for one reason or another, you'll be able to 'achieve' without exchanging money. As mentioned in the book, they can include items that your organisation will underwrite and that therefore won't appear as monetary transactions within the project budget.

2. Assign each item a monetary value. It's sometimes easy to do this, for example if your local church is giving you access to the church hall for one week at no charge but would usually charge a set fee. The amount is often an estimate; for example, if your organisation will be processing all the project funds, the estimated hours at the accountant's usual pay rate will be included in the project's administrative costs.

3. List the items in question, together with their monetary value, in each appropriate section of your project expenditure.

4. List the items in question, again with their monetary value, as part of the project income. On funding bodies' application forms, they often have a section in which they ask you to nominate in-kind support specifically. Ensure you've added the same amounts to both income and expenditure so that the budget remains in balance.

5. Keep a record of the value of your estimated in-kind items so you don't over-extend your allocations when it comes to spending later on!

**Figure 10.2** Checklist: in-kind support.

# Redrafting the budget

We found that we had to redraft the budget for each project on the basis of the funding we secured. We trimmed the project proposal to fit the moneys available and still tried to produce a quality experience for the key artist, the participants and the community audience. You might have to compromise on non-essential budget items, but you also have to allow for contingencies in the form of unexpected expenses, even in the redraft.

Creative ingenuity is vital in budgets too! For the final production week of our *Best Foot Forward* project, for example, project co-artist Christos Linou decided against hiring lighting equipment and personnel; instead, he engaged a teacher from a local tertiary institution to join the production by making the project a learning experience for the teacher's students and asking the teacher to supply the lighting equipment from the stock he used in training his students. Christos acquired the package of expertise and equipment at a negotiated fee within the budget, and the arrangement was another form of support from which mutual benefits flowed.

## Establishing lines of financial accounting

You have to establish clear lines for both managing the project and accounting for the funding. When you're able to identify these clear lines of project management and financial accountability, your chances of being successful in obtaining funding are improved.

Each of the projects in the Community Performance Making Program was jointly managed by the artist and the director, who were advised by the Project Advisory Group. In turn, the director was answerable to the PCLC board for successfully completing the project within an agreed budget and for writing the funding-acquittal report. The day-to-day accounts were administered by a part-time accountant, who was employed at the PCLC on a regular basis.

The PCLC set up the same lines of accounting for all three projects. The key artists were responsible for budgeting for the performance, but the artists' fees were excluded from their area of responsibility: their fees were paid by the accountant either on a fortnightly basis or by way of a timesheet when their hours were limited to completing specific units of work. Pauline Yule, as administrative officer, arranged payment for any expenses incurred after the artists presented an invoice. For small expenses, she set up a petty-cash tin in which a limited 'float' was kept. She increased the amount to an agreed figure during the project's rehearsal and performance stages. The petty cash was routinely reconciled and reimbursed by the same administrative officer.

In Figure 10.3, on page 145, we present a sample balance sheet that we redrafted in line with the project's actual income and expenditure.

Figure 10.3 The
sample balance sheet.

## Sample balance sheet
### Redrafted budget in line with actual income and expenditure

| Income | Budget | Actual |
|---|---|---|
| Government grants: | | |
| • Australia Council: Community Cultural Development Board – New Works | $ 9,600 | $ 9,600 |
| • State government: Arts Victoria | $ 9,975 | – |
| • Local government: Darebin | $ 3,500 | $ 3,500 |
| **Total government grants:** | **$23,075** | **$13,100** |
| | | |
| Direct production income, e.g. box office | $ 2,300 | $ 2,600 |
| Subscriptions and memberships | – | – |
| Donations and business sponsorship, including from the PCLC | $ 3,988 | $ 7,028 |
| Other income: sale of videos | $ 255 | $ 425 |
| | | |
| **Total income:** | **$29,588** | **$23,153** |

| Expenditure | Budget | Actual |
|---|---|---|
| Wages, salaries and fees | | |
| • Artists | $18,230 | $ 15,96 |
| • Other | | $ 824 |
| Direct production costs | $ 5,578 | $ 2,421 |
| Promotional costs | $ 1,245 | $ 747 |
| Administration costs | $ 3,135 | $ 1,801 |
| Other [Please provide details.] | | |
| Documentation (photos, video, reports) | $ 1,400 | $ 1,400 |
| | | |
| **Total expenditure:** | **$29,588** | **$23,153** |
| **Surplus/(Deficit):** | **Nil** | **Nil** |

# Preparing financial statements on a regular basis

During the project's life, it's wise to handle the monetary expenditure by preparing financial statements on a regular basis, and having both the key artist/s and host-organisation manager check them against the budget.

Each financial statement usually includes the artists' fees, the project expenses and an administrative component. Although you can pay some expenses by cheque and some through petty cash, it's critical you establish sound accounting procedures, and that the key artist and host–organisation manager follow them when reconciling the financial statements. When the project concludes, you then have sound evidence that the project has been managed well.

## Evaluating the project

Each project has to be evaluated, both artistically and organisationally. In our case, the artists usually distributed evaluation forms to the participants who completed each workshop and to the people who participated in each performance. People also provided oral feedback in a less formal way. Whenever possible, the artists recorded audience feedback. When we were writing this book, we found all these evaluations to be very valuable.

The evaluations prepared by the arts–team members were also very important, both when we were writing this book and when the PCLC was planning projected strategies. You can obtain this evaluation either orally or in written form, and thereby ensure that it includes reflections on the processes that the organisation has used in support of the project.

It's equally important to undertake financial evaluation of the project, whereby you check the final accounts against the budget and assess what learning you might apply when you're preparing budgets in the future. Two questions you might find yourself asking are:

- Did over–runs occur?
- Were performance ticket prices realistic for offsetting income against expenditure, and did they remain affordable for the local audience at the same time?

## Writing the acquittal report

An acquittal report is written feedback addressed to your funding sources about the way in which the allocated funds were expended. It's also invaluable feedback for fund managers about your project's artistic triumphs and trials.

It's the responsibility of the auspicing body or bodies to be financially accountable to the funding source. The PCLC always required the key artists to view this report as being the final stage in fulfilling their contractual duties; they'd complete the report in co-operation with the centre's director and accountant. The process usually involves attaching a financial statement, in which you've provided details of the project's full and itemised expenditure, to the project's artistic-acquittal report. You won't necessarily have had the financial statement audited when you submit the acquittal report.

## Auditing the financial accounts

A project audit is an external, independent statement of an enterprise's financial accounts. To the best of their ability, auditors guarantee that all the project's income has been appropriately directed and all grant moneys properly spent. When the sums disbursed to the host organisation are sufficiently large, it's sometimes necessary for the organisation to have its financial accounts audited at the end of its financial year (usually 30 June). For example, for grants of $50,000 or more that are disbursed by the Australia Council for the Arts, the accounts have to be audited by a qualified public accountant. A project audit can be conducted during the larger audit of the sponsoring or auspicing organisation after the end of the financial year.

## Preparing the annual report and audited financial statements

The auspicing body or host organisation should include the project audit in its fuller annual report and audited financial statements, and distribute these documents at its annual general meeting, as a component of the lines of accountability it's established in a given community or among defined stakeholders.

It's useful to lodge copies of these printed reports with the funding bodies that disbursed the original grants and to lodge the copies with a covering letter in which you express your appreciation to the funding bodies. Remember to quote your project-grant file number in the letter, so that the funding bodies can reference them easily. Include a photo or two of the project in order to illustrate it visually, if you haven't previously sent visuals with the acquittal report.

In Table 10.1, we present information about our three projects' five budget-related items: funding sources, in-kind support, budget, income, and expenditure.

**Table 10.1** Information about the five budget-related items

| | Once Upon Your Birthday | Spinning, Weaving: Trees and Songs | Best Foot Forward |
|---|---|---|---|
| Funding sources | The Australia Council for the Arts: federal<br><br>Arts Victoria (Vic Arts 21 in 1996): state<br><br>The City of Darebin: local | The Australia Council for the Arts: federal<br><br>The City of Darebin: local<br><br>The City of Darebin: re-mount<br><br>The Preston Uniting Church Parish | The Australia Council for the Arts: federal<br><br>The City of Darebin: local<br><br>The Diana Ferrari Shoe Factory |
| In-kind support | The PCLC | The PCLC<br><br>Re-mount: La Mama Theatre, the PCLC, and the cast members and their friends and relatives | The PCLC<br><br>The Diana Ferrari Shoe Factory |
| Budget | $27,500 | $24,000 | $38,000 |
| Income | $27,476 | $23,153<br>$3000: re-mount | $38,346 |
| Expenditure | $27,476 | $23,156<br>$3000: re-mount | $38,298 |

## Forward planning for your program of community-performance making

To close these chapters in which we've reflected on organisation and management of community-performance projects, we think it's important to note that it's necessary to undertake forward planning in order to retain your program. In chapters 7 to 10, we've outlined the factors that might influence you in your efforts, and discussed the key factors involved in our own program. However, it's important to realise that even the best planning strategy remains subject to outside forces such as economic priorities, social trends, and policies formulated at various levels of successive governments.

Two key outside factors markedly affected how the PCLC's three projects developed most during the period 1995–99. We think that these two factors, as follows, might continue to influence any similar community-arts project.

- Official bodies' arts-policy developments at all levels of government: a significant factor because the bodies are potential funding sources for any community-arts project
- The economic impact of the government's social policy on the local community

The four-year period during which the PCLC was developing its community-arts focus coincided with a period of significant governmental and community change in Victoria and Australia. A 'user pays' principle took hold, and community development, as a model, languished. Small community-arts projects and individual artists often struggled to obtain funding in competition with larger programs and venues.

In forming a vision, the PCLC's board and managers aimed to provide a small oasis for several local artists practising in the performing-arts scene. However, during 1995–99, they found that their ability to sponsor a vibrant performing-arts program for the community was constantly at risk of being compromised due to competing needs both within the centre and externally.

As a result of management scrutiny, they identified that financial pressures existed throughout all the centre's programs and that the pressures were exacerbated by these recognised social factors. To be able to retain the Community Performance Making Program, the PCLC executive members proactively sought solutions from philanthropic trusts and foundations, politicians, and the public.

# Over to you

As we came to the end of writing this book, we reflected on the longer-term benefits of community performance at the PCLC. We realised that a sequence had recurred throughout the three projects: a kind of breathing in and breathing out. All three projects and the Community Performance Making Program as a whole moved through these processes. We've defined the processes as gathering, deepening, and entering into new territory.

## Gathering

In each project, people gathered from many parts of the Preston–Reservoir community. They worked together, arrived at new understandings, and gave a performance. Although the gathering that was specific to each project is long over, it's left its traces in the community in the form of new friendships forged, new networks established, a bit less loneliness and isolation suffered, and a bit more understanding of difference achieved.

## Deepening

During the creative process, there've been inner journeys; sudden realisation of meaning; release of feeling; new connectedness with poetry, dance or story; and a deeper sense of shared humanity. All these experiences were life enriching and life changing.

## Entering into new territory

In each performance, a new work was created and a new statement about what mattered to the Preston–Reservoir community was made. And we realised the potential of using arts processes to engender connection and creativity in places not traditionally viewed as being places for innovation.

## 'Little pockets'

Seeing the impact of community performance in one small host organisation in one locality has been inspiring. It's clear that this type of work can engender personal and social transformation. Within the bigger scheme of things, though, our annual projects are tiny: they involve some hundreds of people among the many thousands living in the Darebin municipality. And they're not extraordinary projects – they're quality examples of work that's going on, in little pockets, all over the country. Australia just needs more little pockets! In our society, more partnerships are needed between organisations, artists and communities so that this work is supported and more people are enriched by it.

The type of participation in artistic processes we've described in this book should be part of the 'bread and butter' of living in a community – not an unusual delicacy. Through engaging in artistic processes, we can enliven and enrich almost every public context of human life, if we can find the structures and forms for the engagement.

Artists shouldn't be isolated and disconnected from the life of their community, as they'd been in Preston–Reservoir. The artist who has a mind for the cultural and political impact of his or her work, the mid-career artist who's looking for connection and replenishment, the tertiary arts graduate who has skills and energy but no employment – all can find a stimulating and life-changing way of engaging with other people by participating in community-arts work.

## 'Natural allies'

Equally, people who work in areas that might seem far removed from the arts world can discover that by engaging in creative processes, they discover a new way of achieving aims and integrating values for themselves as well as for the organisation they work for.

Artists and arts processes are 'natural allies' in health and welfare organisations, in the environment sector, and in both formal and community education. The people involved in these sectors share aims, values and vocabularies with community artists. Arts projects have the potential to fulfil important functions in these areas and to augment existing methods.

It's also possible for community artists and businesses to form relationships of great mutual benefit. Today, within the parameters of corporate culture and business strategies, managers and employees are increasingly accepting the 'triple bottom line' – TBL – method of analysis. The method is predicated on the

qualitative potential of employees and value-adding practices. Its practitioners reject as being anachronistic the solely economic interests evident throughout much of the 1980s and '90s, and instead wish to incorporate, in any analysis, three principles: social accountability, environmental accountability and economic accountability. These TBL businesspeople are looking for legitimate, reciprocal ways to gain entry to their communities. Participating in community-arts work is one of the ways.[38]

The goals of community-performance making are also aligned with the aspirations of many municipal councils. The City of Darebin's Mark Wilkinson explains this affinity:

> Local government is pivotal in the development and encouragement of community participation in the arts. The benefits for the community of this involvement extend beyond the artistic, and are integral in creating harmonious, healthy and vibrant communities. The arts are an important component in establishing what is currently termed the triple bottom line: defining social capital in (1) economic, (2) environmental and (3) social–cultural terms. With this very much in mind, the City of Darebin is keen to foster projects that give voice to people from our diverse community, and we believe that community-arts projects, and performance projects in particular, are an essential ingredient in developing better communities.

## The long-term benefits

In a well-developed and creative collaboration, the outcomes are more than the sum of the parts: what emerges is synergy. All the partners' resources are optimised through the association, and some of each partner's needs can be met through the encounter.

Community-performance making can yield important long-term social, educational, economic and artistic benefits. These benefits are demonstrable in the outcomes achieved. When people patiently invest in community-performance projects, social capital is created.[39]

In Table 11.1, opposite, we list the potential benefits to be gained from collaborating in community-based arts projects. We indicate some of the benefits that flow to each of the potential partners: the community, the host organisation or business, and the artists.

**Table 11.1** The long-term benefits of making art in the community

| For the community | For the host organisation or business | For the artists |
|---|---|---|
| Development and expression of community values | New and effective ways for realising the organisation's existing objectives | The opportunity to express personal values and to contribute to community development |
| Community pride and identity | Improved and broadened relationships with the local community | New creative insights through exposing artforms to new contexts and perspectives |
| Individual self-expression and well-being | An increased public profile | |
| Social cohesion | Association with creative, inclusive community activity | The opportunity to work with and learn from a wide range of people |
| Decreased social isolation | Increased community use of the organisation's facilities | |
| Establishment of community networks | | The opportunity to develop contemporary artwork that's unique to its context |
| Awareness of community issues | An effective way of making contact with people who fall within various demographic groups | A public outcome from the artist's work |
| Better understanding of cultural and lifestyle differences | Access to arts processes as being powerful tools in achieving the aims of community development and community education | The opportunity to engage in sustained work in a supportive environment |
| Increased skills in creativity, communication and community leadership | | The opportunity to develop artistic and community skills in a new context |
| Increased responsibility for collective well-being | Access to arts processes as being powerful tools in achieving the aims of community and individual well-being | Administrative, funding and in-kind support |
| Improved consultation between local government and the community | | Access to office and work space |
| Access to quality arts processes and to creation and viewing of new contemporary performances | Capacity to generate creative public events | Links to other local artists |
| | Partnerships with other organisations, for example local government, businesses or agencies | |

In our experience, when a partnership is formed between the community, the artists and the organisation/s, a 'container', or defined space, is created for the creative process. People come into this safe space; engage deeply with their own experience, emotions and memories; and create artistic form. As a result, personal meaning, personal identity and purpose are built.

However, the process doesn't occur on only an individual level: it contributes both to personal health and well-being and to social health and well-being. Dr Ron Laborte makes the following remarks about this aspect of personal and social health.

> Robert Ornstein and David Sobel in their book *The Healing Brain* claim that the three universal religious principles (respect or caring, generosity or justice, and service to others) are not just good moral principles . . . They are also linked to our own health and well-being, and that of our communities. People who care, who practise justice, who serve others are individually healthier than those who do not. Their actions also create more health for their communities and for the planet. In a profound sense, failure to practise civil behaviour is a serious health hazard, for individuals, communities and societies. It is the 'health message' of the new millennium . . .[40]

Moreover, the process of making a performance requires that we wend together our contributions, stories, movements and insights into a new form through which we communicate with other people. One story 'fires' another. Our individual meanings become part of a formed whole. In the process, we as members of a community begin to articulate social meanings, social values and different points of view that exist in that community. This process entails a rare quality of relationship, listening and collaboration. In clearly expressing what matters to us, we can influence social action, community decision making and social policy.

This is community-building, culture-building work. According to Jon Hawkes:

> Culture is not a pile of artefacts; it is us: the living, breathing sum of us.[41]

This work is one way through which we can, as a society, make a direct, proactive connection between people's living, breathing experience and the social values and actions through which we form the kind of culture we live in. Terry Doyle, the artist who created the Diana Ferrari 'employee of the month' portraits in our *Best Foot Forward* project, makes the following comments about both his involvement in community-art making and his family's efforts to record the small impressions of everyday life.

## Terry's story

*In the* Best Foot Forward *project, a connection was opened between my family and the PCLC. My wife Lucia had a 'first' there: a joint art exhibition of drawings, called Small Impressions. She hadn't shown artwork before. There, she exhibited a series of floral drawings that were then linked with personally meaningful biblical texts.*

*I showed some small watercolour drawings. Half of them were new work, based on photographic references from my box of odd shots that have been accumulating for about thirty years. They were of things seen – and you walk on, then you look back, and think,* That's interesting. *An impression is made. You take the shot. You put it aside for later consideration. The photos were raked over, put together and then drawn. The other half were drawings done over the years and selected as being thematically compatible with Small Impressions.*

*We've had involvement in group art shows. I've exhibited some oil paintings once or twice. In one show, Lucia exhibited a drawing, and our daughter Althea proudly hung one of her watercolours, her first exhibited artwork.*

*Then came the big one: Julie McDonald's Living Newspaper project. We were on this for about fourteen months. It just seemed to go on and on, like a fruitful vine. We were brought together as a group of fifty-pluses – plus one young one later on – to go through the daily papers, extract topics and produce a piece of theatre. This was called Merri Kiss, a collection of six short plays about the experience of older people. Julie coaxed us and coached us and pushed us, and wrote it and directed us, and we performed the piece on 21 to 23 September last year. One of the plays was based on something I wrote. I was touching on drama some thirty years ago, writing and acting, but it faded away. I never thought I'd see something I wrote performed, or ever be on a stage again – but it happened.*

Lucia probably never expected to be on a stage in a play she helped to develop – but there she was, and she did a great job.

Living Newspaper took off in a visual artform, too. Using pages from papers, and charcoal, with Leslie Simpson, we did some drawings. We made our body shapes out of newspaper, and out of papier mache and news headlines, we made newspaper 'heads'. For homework, we had to do a free-choice artwork. I made a printing press. We exhibited these artworks at the PCLC just before the performances. All this paper and print: we owe Johannus Gutenberg a lot – or do we? He's got a lot to answer for.

Somehow, I expect the connection between the PCLC and the Doyle family isn't over with yet.

**Figure 11.1** Terry, at the Art & Soul Gallery.

Figure 11.2 The cast of *Merri Kiss* (left to right): (Front:) Terry Doyle. (First row:) Don Munroe; Lucia Doyle; community artist Julie McDonald; Jean Oakley; Trish Dutton. (Second row:) Robert Tanti; Nicholas Bieber; Leslie Simpson; Mukles Minas; Margaret Tyrrell.

## Merri Kiss

The PCLC is continuing to honour its commitment to making dance and theatre in the community. In 2001, the annual project, *Merri Kiss*, was co-ordinated by the community artist and theatre director Julie McDonald. The project was researched and developed by Darebin residents who were fifty years of age or older. The residents wrote scripts based on personal stories and issues being aired in the media: a daughter's response to her ageing father; older people and information technology; unemployment; relationships; the banks' lack of services; the controversy of euthanasia. The performance was tender, funny and provocative, and the performers offered new values with reference to ageing and the future.

## The 'crucible'

During the writing of this book our – Beth's and Judi's – lives changed course and location: Beth journeyed on to new studies, and Judi moved to a rural city. However, we carry the values and principles of community cultural development with us in our new ventures.

We might be gone, but the PCLC vision goes on: the centre continues to provide opportunities for artists and local residents. In each project, a crucible is created within which community members' creativity can emerge – a personal and community space for transformative processes:

- The time of firing, of facing struggles and refining old understandings
- The safe place in which to be held and to heal
- The vulnerable time of transition and change
- The glimpses of new possibilities

In this way, the old red-brick hall, built in 1894, continues to hold together a narrative and physical environment: the ingredients for community connection. It is one little pocket.

Now it's over to you.

We encourage local communities, artists, community organisations and business interests in Australia to experience the energy, optimism and creativity unleashed in community-performance making.

Go well.

Dare much.

Tell the stories.

Live with the paradoxes.

Experience the illuminating moments of revelation and change.

And succeed surprisingly, relishing the experience of vibrant, inclusive community life.

# Notes

1  Jon Hawkes, for the Cultural Development Network (Victoria). *The Fourth Pillar of Sustainability: Culture's essential role in public planning.*

2  Darebin City Council. *Darebin Community Safety Plan*, 1999–2000 and 2002–03, page 5.

3  Darebin City Council. *Darebin Social Profile*, 1998.

4  State Government of Victoria. Department of Employment, Workplace Relations and Small Business, 1999.

5  In 1998, this community service received major state and federal awards: the VicSafe Award for Violence Reduction, from Victoria's Department of Justice, and a Certificate of Merit in the Australia Violence Prevention Award.

6  On Australia Day (26 January) 1999, in recognition of the PCLC's commitment to community arts and service in the municipality, the centre received the City of Darebin Community Organisation of the Year Award.

7  The quote is from a brochure produced by Community Arts Network (CAN) – South Australia. CAN is the peak body for community arts and has branches in most states, although not Victoria. Its aim is to work 'toward a society in which artistic expression, cultural diversity and human rights are valued and supported'.

8  This area of Melbourne is traditionally Wurundjeri tribal land, and the artwork was created in 1999 by the mosaic artist Maree Clarke in recognition of the connection. In the early days of European settlement, the suburb of Preston was first known as Irishtown, and the bluestone church located on the PCLC site was built during that era.

9  These performance images were originally documented as photographs and colour slides by the photographer Ponch Hawkes. The PCLC also asked Paul Huntingford to shoot video footage, as well as an edited version of the video, which we made available in early 1997. We had another video, of conversations between participants and audience members, made at the end of the project, and it was useful during preparation of this book.

10  For this work, the textile artist and production designer was Ilka White, who's another local artist. The five-panel backdrop was woven by a group of Darebin residents, including Ilka.

11  The backdrop was exhibited in the Annual Wool & Sheep Show in 1998 in Melbourne. Also in 1998, it was used as artwork on the set of *The Sisters Rosensweig*, which was performed by the Williamstown Amateur Theatre Company.

12  We've taken this quote from *Unlaced: A Passion for Shoes*, staged by producer Robyn Ravlich, a self-confessed 'shoe-holic', as quoted on page 44 of *The Age* 'Green Guide', 15 June 2000.

13  The promotional image, as shown in Figure 5.1, was designed by Catrine Berlatier.

14  This worksheet was derived from workshop material offered by Elizabeth Wheeler, a lecturer at the Victorian University of Technology and a project worker with Women's Health Goulburn North East, Victoria. Adapted with permission.

15  For *Best Foot Forward*, for example, students from the Victorian University of Technology's Community Theatre and Small Companies course technically managed the 1999 production, and supplied portable staging, lights and PA equipment.

16  'Dance Forum 2000', in *Communities Dancing*, the journal of Ausdance, the Australian Dance Council.

17  Deidre Williams, *Creating Social Capital: A study of the long-term benefits from community-based arts funding*; available from CAN South Australia.

18  In their evaluations, several participants stated that as a result of their project, they'd gained confidence and insights into themselves. Others stated that they'd learned to work with people who had differing skills and abilities. However, the most profound changes had been the ones through which people's long-held hurts and traumas were eased or healed. It had been possible for this to occur because the person's story was articulated and validated, or he or she developed caring relationships throughout the life of the project.

19  Harold Osborne is an example: he became a skilled weaver in order to help Ilka service and repair the looms that were to be used in the textile project, and he became immersed in the actual shaping of the performance. He joined the storytelling workshop and stayed the distance, which included, in 1998, the return season of *Spinning, Weaving*.

20  Thanks especially to Tim Newth, Ken Conway, Rose Godde, Christos Linou, Mark Wilkinson, Vanessa Case and Bagryana Popov for providing their input for the chapter.

21  In turn, the members of the committee of management were accountable to their original sponsoring body, the local parish council, which comprised representatives of three congregations: High Street, East Preston, and Regent.

22  Immediately afterwards, the exhibition, Paternite, was toured in Queensland at the invitation of a Catholic diocese, and parallel with the exhibition, Dom ran several workshops for men about issues to do with fatherhood, including God's spiritual fatherhood.

23  You may photocopy the checklist when you're using it as a ready checklist for planning your projects. When you're referring to the checklist, please credit the source: Preston Creative Living Centre, *Community Performance Making Program Manual*, 1996.

24  An auspicing body is a third party or organisation that has the legal status of being eligible to consider grant submissions and to agree to do so on an artist's or a project's behalf.

25  The Arts Law Centre of Australia's Web site is <www.artslaw.asn.au/~artslaw>; its e-mail address is <artslaw@artslaw.asn.au>; its postal address is The Gunnery, 43–51 Cowper Wharf Road, Woolloomooloo, New South Wales 2011; and its phone numbers are (02) 9356 2566 or toll free 1800 221 457.

26  At the time of writing of the book, these facts were as accurate as possible. Although we've established categories of information for supporting our projects, the details such as fee schedules can alter over time and from location to location. It's necessary to seek updated information for each project.

27  WorkCover representatives provide helpful advice when you contact them about a specific employment situation.

28  With reference to income and expenditure, it's worth obtaining a copy of the pamphlet 'Performing Artists' from your nearest Australian Taxation Office or at the Web site <www.ato.gov.au>.

29  The Australia Council for the Arts has excellent and current information about community-arts copyright, and the information is available on request: phone (02) 9950 9000 or toll free 1800 226 912, or visit the Web site <www.ozco.gov.au>. Another useful source of information is the Australian Copyright Council: visit the Web site <www.copyright.org.au>; e-mail <cpright@copyright.org.au>; phone (02) 9318 1788; or write to 4/245 Chalmers Street, Redfern, New South Wales 2016.

30  The publication entitled *Copyright and Community Arts* is one resource available from the Australia Council for the Arts. It contains a clear overview of the issues as well as referrals to other useful resources.

31 For more information, visit the federal government's Web site <www.privacy.gov.au> or your state or territory government's site, such as, for Victoria, <www.privacy.vic.gov.au>.

32 You can access this collection of books, reports, videos, slides, flyers and so on by visiting the Web site <www.vca.unimelb.edu.au/ library/carc/index.html>.

33 You may photocopy the checklist when you're using it as a ready checklist for planning your projects. When you're referring to the checklist, please credit the source: Preston Creative Living Centre, *Community Performance Making Program Manual*, 1996.

34 This hasn't occurred on only one occasion: in our 1999 project, we chose the theme of 'living newspapers' in applying to the City of Darebin for a conceptual grant before we'd negotiated with a key artist.

35 The Australian Taxation Office's publication *Arts and Culture: The New Tax System*, second edition, revised in May 2000, is a good resource.

36 *The Australian Directory of Philanthropy* is a good resource to access through libraries or to purchase for your own use. It's published by Philanthropy Australia Inc., located at Level 10, 530 Collins Street, Melbourne, Victoria 3000. As at April 2001, it could be purchased for $45 through the organisation's bookshop. For more details, see 'Selected resources', on page 182.

37 At the time of writing, Mark was responsible for developing the City of Darebin's arts policy and program as well as its arts and cultural infrastructure. He was also lecturing in arts management at the Victorian College of the Arts, located at The University of Melbourne.

38 To gain a sense of the multiplicity of contexts of community-arts work, see Appendix C for a list of arts projects that the Australia Council for the Arts's Community Cultural Development Board funded between 2000 and 2001.

39 Deidre Williams. *Creating Social Capital: A study of the long-term benefits from community based arts funding.*

40 Dr Ron Laborte. *Power, Participation and Partnerships for Health Promotion.* Carlton South: VicHealth, 1997; 'Chapter 5: Power and Empowerment: Building Transformative Relations from the Inside Out', page 40.

41 Jon Hawkes, for the Cultural Development Network (Victoria). *The Fourth Pillar of Sustainability: Culture's essential role in public planning.*

# Appendix A Biographies of the project key artists and key contributors to the book

## Vanessa Case

Vanessa is a dancer, teacher and choreographer, and is widely experienced in the fields of creative and improvised dance. She studied ballet as a child, and while studying for her Bachelor of Arts degree and Diploma of Education at The University of Melbourne, was introduced to contemporary dance through the Guild Dance Theatre. She went on to complete a Graduate Diploma in Movement and Dance, through which she broadened her awareness of community–dance issues, especially in relation to children and people who have a disability.

Vanessa has worked as a street performer and an improviser, has studied with the Lieto Dance School, and has taught dance classes for parents and multi-age participants, from toddlers to elderly people. She's choreographed several musicals, including, in 1996, a spectacular staged at Heatherwood Special School.

In 1998–99, she was co-artistic director of the PCLC's *Best Foot Forward* project. In 2000, she was a member of the Victorian delegation to the first Community Dance Conference, held in Sydney. She's worked with teenagers in the Dance and Well-Being program conducted through the City of Moreland, as well as with elderly Chinese and Italian migrant women, in association with Women's Health in the North and the City of Darebin.

## Judi Fisher

Judi was the PCLC's director from 1995 to 1999. During her five-year tenure, she initiated the centre's Community Performance Making Program, which was originally known as the Artist-in-Residence Program. She obtained funding for three artist-in-residence projects, for which her responsibilities were organisational supervision and accountability.

In 2000, Judi and Beth were hired by the PCLC to undertake this performing-arts publication project, *Face to Face*, funded through the Community Cultural Development Board of the Australia Council for the Arts. From August 2000 to July 2002, she worked as promotions and publications officer on a part-time basis for the regional Victorian organisation Women's Health Goulburn North East. She continues to freelance as a writer and an editor.

Judi's interest in nurturing visual and performing artists emerged between 1985 and 1989, when she was chaplain at the Royal Melbourne Institute of Technology (now RMIT University). In 1993, she documented a unique arts project, in which the Uniting Church in Australia commissioned several Australian painters to create contemporary and inclusive images based on Leonardo da Vinci's *The Last Supper*. With Janet Wood, she co-authored *A Place at the Table: Women at the Last Supper*, as a record of this project; the book was published by the Australian Christian Literature Society and was a finalist in the

1994 Book of the Year Awards. *A Place at the Table* is now out of print; however, it was well received in Australia, New Zealand and Canada.

Judi's first career was in teaching, in Papua New Guinea, the United States and Vanuatu. Between 1981 and 1985, she was national officer of the Women and Development Network in Australia, and she's been an editorial-board member for the youth magazine *A.D.* In 1986–87, she was a founding officer of and the editor for the Tertiary Campus Ministry Association of Australia. In 1998–99, she was a community-agency member of the City of Darebin's Safer Communities Steering Committee. She continues to have wide-ranging interests and to participate in community forums.

## Christos Linou

Christos is a Melbourne-based choreographer, performer and production director, and has worked with companies located in Cyprus, London and Amsterdam. In 1998–99, he was co-artistic director of the PCLC's *Best Foot Forward* project, for which he initiated and negotiated the community-arts partnership with the Diana Ferrari Shoe Factory. In 2000, he was artist-in-residence at the Footscray Community Arts Centre. He's now Vice Chairperson of Dancehouse.

Christos commenced his dancing career in Adelaide at age twenty-two, and continues to follow three main interests: bold and innovative form, human nature, and social complexities. He studied at Adelaide's Centre for Performing Arts, and completed his studies in 1987. Although he's a trained classical dancer, he energetically pursues work that lies on the boundaries between dance and other artforms, by collaborating with filmmakers, writers and visual artists.

In Australia, his performance work has included *Days and Nights with Christ* and *To Traverse Water*, for the IHOS Opera, in 1997; *Magdalena,* for the Ballarat Opera, in 1996; *Little Red Wood*, for the Green Mill Dance Project; and *Full Flight*, for Dancehouse. He's also experienced in presenting large-scale community-arts projects, such as the Moving Line Community Dance Project, which he staged in 1996 in Albury, New South Wales, with ten regional schools.

His non-dance skills include fluency in the Modern Greek language, photography, film, teaching and stage management. In Adelaide, he's also worked on creating art and music activities for disadvantaged young offenders.

## Alice Nash

Alice is a community-arts worker. She's skilled in project administration, theatre production and design, and she's co-ordinated and managed festivals and theatre projects and organisations located in Australia and Canada. In 1997, she was project facilitator and an arts-team member for the PCLC's *Spinning, Weaving: Trees and Songs* project. She was involved in the project's conceptual stage and the series of storytelling workshops through which the performance was eventually built.

Alice writes and speaks English, French and Russian. In 1992, she studied at Moscow State University. In 1993, she was awarded a Bachelor of Arts degree, with Honours and Distinction, in Russian and French Language and Literature, from The University of Alberta, Canada.

Since arriving in Melbourne, Alice has held co-ordination positions with the 1996 Melbourne Fringe Festival, the Melbourne Moomba Festival and the Big West Festival, and has worked on a myriad of independent theatre projects.

Alice has performed with the Brunswick Women's Theatre, in the production *Routine and Ritual*. Most recently, she was General Manager of Geelong's Back to Back Theatre, and is now Associate Producer of Performance with Melbourne's Next Wave Festival.

## Bagryana Popov

Bagryana is a theatre creator, a performer and a producer of new work. In 1996, she directed the choir and vocals for the PCLC's *Once Upon Your Brithday* project. In 1997, she was the PCLC's key artist for the centre's *Spinning, Weaving: Trees and Songs* project. She shaped and directed the final production of *Spinning, Weaving*, which in September 1998 was re-mounted for a highly successful five-day season at the Carlton Courthouse Theatre.

Since graduating from the Victorian College of the Arts, Bagryana has been involved in several theatre productions, including *Woman in the Wall* and *The Wedding* for the Hildegard Theatre group, of which she's a founding member. In 1995–96, the group worked in collaboration with *avant garde* Bulgarian theatre artists to create the production *Inje*, a work that was performed in both Bulgaria and Australia, through Theatreworks.

Bagryana has created a series of solo performances, the first of which, *White Nada*, was based on a Bulgarian folk tale and was staged at La Mama Theatre, for the Melbourne Fringe Festival. She's also performed with other companies and artists, in *The Olive Tree*, for the 1990 Adelaide Festival; *The Trojan Woman*, in 1992; *Blood Moon*, in 1998; and Chekov's *Three Sisters*, in 1997.

From 1992 to the present, she's been musical director of the award-winning women's choir Petrunka. The choir has performed extensively in Australia, in Bulgaria and Hungary, and at several festivals. More recently, her involvement in community-arts performances has included directing *Hags, Hair and Leeches*, for the City of Darebin, and a theatre piece for Melbourne's Immigration Museum. She's now the Victorian member of the Community Cultural Development Board of the Australia Council for the Arts.

## Beth Shelton

Beth is a choreographer and psychologist, and is completing doctoral studies at Swinburne University. She began her professional life as a founding member of the Danceworks dance company, and was the company's co-artistic director from 1989 to '91. She spent fifteen years choreographing dance works in dance companies and communities throughout Australia. Her works have included *One Meets Two Parts*, *Tide* and *Common Touch*, for Danceworks, and *Groundswell* and *Time Present*, for Tasdance. Her large-scale community-performance projects have included *Going Dancing*, in 1986; *Dance on Darwin*, in 1989; *Wings of Summer*, in 1990 and '91; and *Once Upon Your Birthday*, at the PCLC, in 1996. She's also worked often with the Tracks dance company in Darwin.

Beth has taught in many of Australia's tertiary dance courses. She's been the recipient of Australia Council travel–study grants, and studied in New York and London. From 1993 to '96, she chaired the Dance Advisory Panel of Victoria's Ministry for the Arts. Her writing is included in the books *If you can move you can dance*, published in 1994, and *Dancers and Communities*, published in 1997. She co-facilitated *Moving On 2000*, Australia's first national gathering of community-dance workers.

In Beth's work, she combines her interests in dance and bodily experience, psychology and community.

# Appendix B The people who performed in the three projects

Please note that as much as humanly possible, we've tried to list people's full names and the roles they had in each project. In some instances, the person chose not to reveal his or her full identity, and in others, the names weren't fully recorded.

## Once Upon Your Birthday, 1996

### The performers and storytellers

Darielle Crawford and Ryan Taplin: aerial duo
Marina Bistrin: oriental dancer
Stephanie Francis: jester and sprite
Rhea Dempsey: midwife and angel
Julie Perrin: storyteller
Cass Kiely: child
Jane Bayley: singer and composer of 'Jump'
Madeline Flynn, Tim Humphrey and
   Clare de Bruin: musicians
Rinski Ginsberg: make-up
Mothers' and babies' group
Parents' and children's group
Storytellers' group
Midwives' group
Petrunka: choir
Ghanaian drummers and dancers
Pontian-Greek dancers
East Preston Uniting Church drummers
High Street Uniting Church 'gift givers'
Riga Academy ballet students
Preston Neighbourhood House playgroup

### The arts-team members

Beth Shelton: director, choreographer,
   production manager and researcher
Mahoney Kiely: assistant director, and visual
   and fire artist
Stephanie Francis: production assistant and
   publicist
Julie Perrin: community-storytelling
   co-ordinator
Bagryana Popov: Musical director of Petrunka:
   The Melbourne Women's Bulgarian Choir
Clare de Bruin: community drum-band
   co-ordinator
Tina Baggio: graphic designer of poster and
   logo

### The documentation providers

Ponch Hawkes and Judi Fisher: photographers
Paul Huntingford: video artist

## Spinning, Weaving: Trees and Songs, 1997

### The arts-team members

Bagryana Popov: community artist and artistic
   director
Ilka White: project designer and textile artist
Alice Nash: workshop facilitator and publicist
   (for phase one: March to May)
Deborah Hatton: facilitator, publicist, lighting
   designer and stage manager (for phase two:
   September to December)

## The performers and storytellers

Gordana Garment
Glenys Janssen
Emilia Maubach
Mukles Minas
Harold Osborne
Eva Popov
Ria Soemardjo
Andrew Compton
Norm Davis
Nance Davis
Margaret Johnson
Wally Johnson
Cliff Scott
Geraldine Bate
Nancy Black
Sharon Dewar
Judith Dodds
Gillian Essex
Janice Florence
Edwina Harrison
Ann Howard
Cleo Macmillan
Lisa Sulinski
Therese Virtue
Ilka White
Petrunka: The Melbourne Women's Bulgarian
   Choir

## The spinners, weavers and designers

Twenty-two spinners and weavers were
contacted individually and through the
Spinners' Guild. Five looms and ten spinning
wheels were involved in the actual process, and
the wool skeins were hand dyed on site.

The weavers were Joan Dever, Harold
Osborne, Glenys Janssen, Kristen Beggs, Lisa
Baker, Judith Dodds, Chris Courtney, and
Sharon Dewar.

The spinners were Nita Discoll, Betty Brun,
Eleanor Foster, Cleo Macmillan, Therese
Virtue, Ida Comport, Pana Yota, Melanie
Priede, Jan, Sarah, Inez, Joamy Smith, Edwina
Harrison, and Janine. The canvas flats used in
the stage design were painted by Terry White
and Tali White.

The Northcote Preston Helping Hand
Association, its members and its artist Olga
Murray hand made the program covers and
printed the posters.

## The visual artists

Ilka White: graphic designer of logo
Visual artists from the NEAMI Inc. (previously
   the North East Alliance for the Mentally Ill)
   Splash Arts Studio, located in High Street,
   Reservoir
One Aboriginal artist
Owners of precious family photos, albums, old
   books, school prizes, ration cards, and local
   and family memorabilia

## The involved community groups

An English-language class from Acacia College
An English-language class from the Preston
   Adult Migrant Education Service (AMES)
Three congregations and two clergy members
   from the Preston Uniting Church Parish
The University of the Third Age (U3A),
   Thornbury
The Iraqi Women's Association
The Northcote–Preston Helping Hand
   Association
Harry Thompson from MIText
The Jika Jika Community Centre
The Brotherhood of St Laurence

## The documentation providers

Kyla Jane Hunt and Judi Fisher: photographers

## Best Foot Forward, 1998–99

### The arts-team members
Vanessa Case: community artist
Christos Linou: performance director
Liz Landray: music composer
Robyn Shannon: visual artist
Marina Bistrin: art worker
Caterine Berlatier: designer (1998 only)
Deborah Kanaghinis: core member (1998 only)

### The performers and storytellers
Trish and Tess Devlin
Emma Greenwood
Mukles Minas
Sissy Morrow
Maria Sapounas
Summi and Niroshan
Lucy Taylor
Natalea Iskra
Liliana Bosancic
Clare Nugent
Bill Hurley
Vito Celestino
Leanne Sheriff
Carla De Fazio
Vicky Rousis
Tony Depetro
Ray Drew
Margi Coe
Debra England
Susie Novak
Mathew Rodoreda
Steven
Michelle Toffe
Freda
Helen Burbach
Bronya Gibson
Chris Stamkovski and the Macedonian
 Senior Citizens Dance Group
Steve Sotiriou and the Pegas Dance Academy

Poppy Papmikroulis and the Sabath Dance
 Group
Belinda Wong
Athena Saliacos

### The visual artists
Catrine Berlatier: graphic designer of the logo
Terry Doyle: painter, The Shoemaker
 exhibition
Students from Thornbury Primary, Preston
 Primary, East Preston Primary and North
 East Preston Primary schools: creators of the
 backdrops
Students from the Preston Special
 Developmental School: creators of artwork
Leisure Action: contributors of the banners
Christos Linou and Geoffrey Moore: creators
 of the float
Robyn Shannon: creator of the red-stiletto
 prop and other shoe images (shoes donated
 by the Australian Ballet, the National Trust,
 Thornbury Lions Club and various people)

### The publicity and promotion contributors
Stephanie Francis and Leader Community
 Newspapers (Northern Division)
Radio 3CR
*D'Art* magazine
Barbara Doherty
Brenda MacDonald
Monica Tessalaar

### The providers of technical and lighting support
Greg Dyson
Victoria University of Technology
 (Community Theatre – Sunbury Campus)

## The documentation providers

George Mifsud, Christos Linou and
  Judi Fisher: photographers
Christos Linou: filmmaker
Vanessa Case: video maker

## The providers of in-kind support

The managers and staff members of the
  Diana Ferrari Shoe Factory, especially
  Charles Cutajar
Lucia Doyle and family
Kirralee Enders and Malcolm
Zoe Linou and Janet Williams
Leisure Action, including Teresa Micallef
MS8FG
Dancehouse
Ausdance
Catrine Berlatier, DAAG House (The Darebin
  Artists' Action Group Inc.)
Darebin Festival
Marcus Roberts
Shara Poole
The Great Darebin Music Expo
Kylie Wilkinson
Dean Linguey
Carol McBain and reflexology students
Sue Hannaford
Steve Fioretti
Reverend Wally Johnson
KUCA Kindergarten
Bronwyn Ritchie
Lilianz Designs
Mark Wilkinson (City of Darebin)
Betty Landray
Stephanie Glickman

# Appendix C The timeframes and budgets for the three projects

## Once Upon Your Birthday, 1996
### Timeframe

|  | Research and community contact | Community process and rehearsal | Performance | Evaluation |
|---|---|---|---|---|
| Length | 12 weeks | 6 weeks | 2 weeks | 3 days |
| Beth | 2 days per week | 3 days per week | 2 weeks full time | 3 days |
| Other artists |  | Variable | 2 weeks full time | 1 day |

### Budget

**Income**

| | |
|---|---|
| Australia Council for the Arts: federal government | |
| Community Cultural Development Fund – New Work | $ 9,950 |
| Arts Victoria (then Vic Arts 21): state government | $ 8,100 |
| City of Darebin: local government | $ 2,805 |
| PCLC: in-kind support | $ 5,000 |
| Sponsorship | $ 595 |
| Box office | $ 1,026 |
| Total income: | $27,476 |

**Expenditure**

| | |
|---|---|
| Community artists' fees, including on-costs | $10,514 |
| Performance artists' fees and assistance | $ 6,764 |
| Direct costs: performance | $ 5,710 |
| Overheads | $ 2,293 |
| Publicity | $ 795 |
| Documentation | $ 1,400 |
| Total expenditure: | $27,476 |
| Balance: | Nil |

# Spinning, Weaving: Trees and Songs, 1997

## Timeframe

|  | Conceptual and workshopping | Workshopping | Rehearsal | Evaluation | Re-mount |
|---|---|---|---|---|---|
| Length | 12 weeks (24 days) | 11 weeks (25 days) | 2 weeks | 4 days | 5 days |
| Bagryana | 2 days per week | 2 to 3 days per week | Full time | 4 days | 1 month |
| Ilka | Half day per week | 1 to 2 days per week | Full time | 2 days | 10 days |
| Alice | Half day per week | 1 day per week | – | – | – |
| Deb |  | 1 day per week | Full time | – | – |
| Other artists |  | Variable | Variable | 1 day | – |
| Total: 65 days |  |  | Performance: 29 and 30 November 1997 |  | September 1998 |

## Budget

### Income

| | |
|---|---|
| Australia Council for the Arts: federal government | |
| Community Cultural Development Fund – New Work | $ 9,600 |
| City of Darebin: local government – initial project | $ 3,500 |
| PCLC: in-kind support | $ 7,028 |
| Box office | $ 2,600 |
| Sale of story booklets and videos | $     425 |
| Total income: | $ 23,153 |
| | |
| City of Darebin: *theatre re-mount | $ 3,000 |

### Expenditure

| | |
|---|---|
| Community artists' fees, including on–costs | $ 15,960 |
| Other wages and fees | $     824 |
| Direct costs: performances | $ 2,421 |
| Overheads | $ 1,804 |
| Promotion and publicity | $     747 |
| Documentation | $ 1,400 |
| Total expenditure: | $ 23,156 |

\* In 1998, the City of Darebin again sponsored the full re-mounting of the production. The performance had a limited, five-night season at the Carlton Courthouse Theatre, under the auspices of La Mama Theatre, and the performers played to full houses. The $3000 for the re-mount was fully spent. It's worth noting that $3000 is an extremely lean budget for a re-mount, and that the Darebin grant was supplemented through a lot of other in-kind generosity, from La Mama Theatre, the PCLC, and the cast members and their friends and relatives.

## Best Foot Forward, 1998–99

### Timeframe

|  | April 1998 | November 1998 | December 1998 | June 1999 | October 1999 | November 1999 |
|---|---|---|---|---|---|---|
| Length: 18 months | *A Toe in the Water* | The Shoes with Soul exhibition | Christmas celebration | The Shoemaker exhibition | *Ankle High* | *Stepping Out with Your Best Foot Forward* |
| Vanessa | – | – | – | Red Shoe Day | – | – |
| Christos | – | – | – | – | – | – |

### Budget, for the eighteen-month project

**Income**

| | |
|---|---|
| Australia Council for the Arts: federal government | |
| Community Cultural Development Fund – New Work | $ 28,500 |
| City of Darebin: local government | $  4,900 |
| PCLC: in-kind support | $  3,207 |
| Box office | $    277 |
| Sponsorship and donations: the Diana Ferrari Shoe Factory | $  1,462 |
| Total income: | $ 38,346 |

**Expenditure**

| | |
|---|---|
| Community artists' fees, including on-costs | $ 20,388 |
| Other wages and fees | $  2,753 |
| Direct costs: performances | $  8,968 |
| Overheads | $  2,726 |
| Promotion and documentation | $  3,463 |
| Total expenditure: | $ 38,298 |

# Appendix D Selected Australia Council Community Cultural Development Fund projects

In this table, we include a selected list of performance projects funded in 2000–01 through the Community Cultural Development Fund of the Australia Council for the Arts. We're including the list to demonstrate the many contexts in which community performance is used and the range of funding that's approved.

| Grant recipient | Title of project | Description | Funding granted |
|---|---|---|---|
| Adelaide Lesbian and Gay Festival | *Black 'n' Out* | A work created by indigenous artists | $23,200 |
| African Women's Performing Arts Project | | A performance work; looking at communication issues for African women | $40,000 |
| | *All My Love* | Exploration and documentation of love stories from older people | $23,000 |
| Arts Are Access | | A multi-artform project; workshops and performance involving people who had a disability | $7,000 |
| Back to Back Theatre Inc. | *Fishman* | A community-theatre performance by people who had a disability as well as by able-bodied performers | $19,620 |
| Brunswick Women's Theatre | *Stories and Symbols* | A community-developed performance; exploring personal and cultural storytelling | $55,380 |

| Grant recipient | Title of project | Description | Funding granted |
| --- | --- | --- | --- |
| The 'Camp Have a Chat' and 'Let's Talk' Project | | A residential theatre workshop for youths and their families from a non-English speaking background | $6,738 |
| Cascade Place (Cerebral Palsy League of Queensland) | *A Garden on the Moon* | A performance project involving people who had a disability | $33,015 |
| CERES | *Kingfisher Incarnation* | Performance for the seventh annual Return of the Sacred Kingfisher festival | $12,000 |
| Citymoon Theatre | *Finding the Buffalo* | A performance about cultural identity | $20,000 |
| Corrugated Iron Youth Arts Inc. | *2D Stage One* | Creating a model for teaching circus across cultures and developing performance pieces | $27,486 |
| Crossroads Arts | | Workshops leading to performance and exhibition by people who had a disability | $13,036 |
| D Faces of Youth Arts Inc. | *www.licensed2.com/ municat* | A multimedia theatrical production | $49,000 |
| DADAA (Western Australia) Inc. | *Exile* | A large-scale performance involving people who had a disability | $27,500 |
| Dale Street Women's Community Centre | | Forum theatre for young people to explore issues of violence against women | $49,136 |
| Damarko, Antonio | *Pluralia* | A ritual–theatrical production involving young people from a non-English speaking background | $14,960 |

| Grant recipient | Title of project | Description | Funding granted |
| --- | --- | --- | --- |
| East African Playgroup | *Wazee Hukumbuka* | A storytelling project in which members of Melbourne's African community were brought together | $20,504 |
| Gasworks Arts Inc. | *Gasworks Performance Skills Project* | Skills development for people who had a disability as well as for senior citizens | $20,000 |
| Horizon Theatre Co. Ltd | *School of Puppetry and Visual Arts* | For multicultural youth | $31,775 |
| Horn of African Community Network Arts Committee | | Music–theatre performances featuring communities from the Horn of Africa | $25,000 |
| Hothouse Theatre | *Burn!* | A collaborative musical-theatre project | $49,657 |
| In Transit | | Four women from a non-English speaking background developing a community-theatre piece with the Riverina Theatre Company | $15,905 |
| Junction House Inc. | | A musical produced collaboratively by people who had a disability | $27,532 |
| Kalamunda Zig Zag Festival | *Welcoming the Future* | A ceremony in celebration of the International Year of the Culture of Peace | $23,040 |

| Grant recipient | Title of project | Description | Funding granted |
| --- | --- | --- | --- |
| Karen Community Theatre Project | | A community-theatre project featuring Melbourne's Karen community | $34,700 |
| Kununurra Youth Service | | Workshops for developing skills in the visual and performing arts, undertaken with remote communities in Australia's eastern Kimberley region | $20,000 |
| Maribyrnong Festival Pty Ltd | *Our Backyard* | A community dance and music event for the Big West Festival | $25,991 |
| Mikhail, Samia | | A multimedia stage performance for the Arabic-speaking community | $20,000 |
| Moreland Community Health Services | | A multimedia performance and exhibition for Melbourne's Next Wave Festival | $40,000 |
| Multicultural Women's Network | *Stirring the Pot* | Production and presentation of a cross-cultural performance | $43,330 |
| Newcastle Maritime Museum Society Inc. | *Sealed with all my love* | A storytelling and installation project | $12,375 |
| PACT Youth Theatre | *Stand Your Ground* | A community site-based performance | $40,700 |
| Paradigm Productions | *The Grand Feeling* | A 'storytelling and mixed-media play' project by elders from the community | $39,857 |
| Ponnor, Cicily | *Frontiers* | A performance piece; exploring the Green Valley community | $2,000 |

| Grant recipient | Title of project | Description | Funding granted |
|---|---|---|---|
| Preston Creative Living Centre Inc. | *The Living Newspaper* | A theatre, visual-arts and debate project | $32,000 |
| Restless Dance Company | *Lifespan* | A community-dance program; working with people who had an intellectual disability | $27,000 |
| Riverland Youth Theatre Inc. | *Red Light Running* | A youth-theatre production; targeting depression, risk taking and identity | $11,000 |
| Roma and District Community Support Association | | An introduction to the language of community theatre, leading to an established youth drop-in centre | $8,320 |
| Somebody's Daughter Theatre Inc. | | New, multi-dimensional work, undertaken with three marginalised communities | $50,000 |
| The Silver Sirens | *Higher Ground* | A musical-theatre piece; examining drug and alcohol abuse in the local community | $25,000 |
| Theatreworks Ltd | *Designer Child* | An integrated drama project | $13,500 |
| Urban Theatre Projects Ltd | *Camp Villawood* | A site-based community performance | $47,432 |
| Vulcana Women's Circus | | Two physical-theatre pieces for the Reclaim the Night event | $47,300 |
| Weave Movement Theatre | | Development, production and performance of a community-dance piece | $16, 469 |
| Y3P Young People's Performance Projects | *Rites of Passage* | A theatre performance staged by young people | $40,000 |

# Acknowledgements

I'm an avid book reader, and I've spent many years checking out acknowledgement pages. I'm intrigued by what they either reveal or conceal: perhaps a warm tone of writing; an inclusive and comprehensive format; erudition of meticulous researchers; sense of humour, friendliness and personality; the easily recognisable arrogant voice; one author's limited words mirrored against the expression of another's reflective, private soul. – Judi

Now it's our turn to thank the many individual people and organisation representatives who, between 1995 and 2001, participated in the Preston Creative Living Centre's (PCLC's) projects and/or the writing of this book. It's a daunting task: what if we've missed someone? If we have, we apologise in advance!

Every project has partners, and partnership is one of the themes of the book and of the community-arts projects we examine. In the following acknowledgements, we credit our partners.

## The project participants

First and foremost, we thank the energetic, adventurous, committed and creative people who participated in *Once Upon Your Birthday, Spinning, Weaving: Trees and Songs* and *Best Foot Forward*. They were the heart and soul of the three projects, and were a major source of our inspiration for writing this book.

## The community artists

We owe a special debt of thanks to the community artists who were our immediate partners in the projects: Bagryana Popov from *Spinning, Weaving: Trees and Songs*, and Vanessa Case and Christos Linou from *Best Foot Forward*, each of whom wrote material for this book. Other community artists and participants in the three projects have generously permitted us to use their material. Thank you for giving us your rich donation of time, encouragement and memories in bringing this book to life.

## The sponsoring body

We wish to thank the members of the PCLC's sponsoring body, the Preston Uniting Church Parish. We could never adequately acknowledge how willing they were to both risk this new venture in ministry and 'walk the talk' about investing in their surrounding community by way of supporting the centre's arts programs and family-violence service. Now, a decade later, we can reflect on their human and financial gift, on the journey's triumphs and pains, on its potential, and on its realisation.

We especially wish to extend our appreciation to the PCLC Board of Management for supporting the Community Performance Making Program between 1996 and 2001. In particular, we thank the executive board members from those years: Rosalyn Strongman, Pauline Gibbs, John Anderson, Jack Hollaway and Carol McBain.

## The host-organisation staff members

We thank the current staff members, both paid and volunteer – they also represent other staff members, over various projects' lifetimes, who through their presence at the PCLC have contributed to the success of each project. We thank you for 'being PCLC': the face of the centre's diversity, warmth, care, challenge and affirmation in the community.

We especially acknowledge the following PCLC staff members who over the past eighteen months have supported the writing and the later stages of the book's publication: director Veronica Rodenburg, administrative officers Pauline Yule and Kathy Beckwith, accountant Yvonne Coutts, and family-violence intervention program co-ordinator Andrew Compton.

## The funding bodies

We wish to thank the funding bodies through which the PCLC's Community Performance Making Program was made possible: the Community Cultural Development Board of the Australia Council for the Arts, for substantially financially backing the individual projects between 1996 and 2001, and for providing the funding through which we were able to realise the book; the City of Darebin, for providing community grants and enabling us to work with key staff members between 1995 and 2001: Community Arts Officer Carol Mavric, and Arts and Cultural Officer Mark Wilkinson; Arts Victoria, for providing funding in 1996; and the members of the Morris Family Trust (Perpetual Trustees), for providing support for gallery exhibitions throughout the 1998 stage of the *Best Foot Forward* project.

## The industry partner

We wish to credit our 1998–99 partner the Diana Ferrari Shoe Factory, the factory's owner Tony Kirkhope and the factory's employees for allowing us to enter their industry and workspace and hear their stories. We especially thank Charles Cutajar, who became the linchpin between the factory and the PCLC, and we also wish to thank the visual artist Terry Doyle.

## The two church networks

During the period we cover in the book, the PCLC's work was supported through collegial encouragement and exchange of resources and information provided by two distinct networks: the Uniting Church creative living and learning centres (the Augustine Centre – Hawthorn; the Centre for Creative Ministries – East St Kilda; the Chalice – Northcote; the Richmond Creative Living Centre; and the Otira Centre – Kew) and the North-West Federation of Uniting*Care* (the north-western Melbourne community services of the Uniting Church in Australia: Broadmeadows CARE; Kildonan Child and Family Services; Moreland Hall Drug and Alcohol Rehabilitation Centre; and Orana Family Services).

## The book advisory group

We thank the members of the book advisory group: the author and theatre director-producer Meme McDonald, for giving us her timely advice at critical points and for writing the foreword to the book, and the PCLC's current director Veronica Rodenburg, who's been both a colleague of ours and the link between the writing project and the PCLC.

We also thank Heather Broadfoot, Alice Nash and Mark Wilkinson for their constructive comments on drafts of the book. Alice Nash also researched the material in Appendix D and the selected resources.

## The publishing house

We express our heartfelt appreciation to the directors and staff members of our publisher, Spinifex Press, who saw value in both our manuscript and our dreams for community performing arts: publishers Susan Hawthorne and Renate Klein; editor Deb Doyle; designer Deb Snibson; publicity and promotions co-ordinator Johanna De Wever; and office manager Maralann Damiano.

## Our family members

Finally, we want to dip our hats to our family members, who had to rearrange their lives and activities many times during the performance and publication projects. Rex and Jaom Fisher, and Ian, Brenna and Alex Ferguson loved us during every stage and cheered us on to complete the task.

We've made every effort to seek permission to quote all the participants whose words we've reproduced. We regret if we've been unable to seek your permission due to your travels, change of address or life circumstances.

**Preston Creative Living Centre**

Australia Council
for the Arts

This project has been assisted by the Commonwealth Government through the Australia Council, its arts funding and advisory body.

The research and writing of this publication have been assisted by the City of Darebin through its Community Grant Scheme.

# Selected resources

## Australia Council for the Arts resources and publications

*Copyright and Community Arts.*
A guide to establishing ownership of creative works produced by artists and communities, and contacts for more advice.

*Hands On, 2000.*
A guide to the grants programs of the Community Cultural Development Board. Each program is illustrated with examples to provide insight into some of the activities and outcomes generated from community cultural development work.

*Access All Areas,* 1999.
A practical, clear guide to improving your organisation and opening your doors to the whole of the community.

*Australia Council Support for the Arts Handbook.* Published annually.
An outline of the Australia Council's grant programs, and a list of key Australia-wide organisations, included in the section entitled 'Arts Resource Organisations'.

## Resources from the field

Australian Taxation Office. *Arts and Culture: The New Tax System.* Second edition. Commonwealth of Australia, 2000.
A brief introduction to Australia's new taxation system, including an explanation of GST entitlements and obligations as well as accounting for GST.

Australian Taxation Office. *Performing Artists, 1999–2000.* NAT 2324 06.2000.
Details about tax deductions for employee performing artists.

Binns, Vivienne (editor). *Community and the Arts: History, Theory, Practice.* Pluto Press, 1991.
A series of essays in which the aim is to provide the beginnings of a history and theory of Australian community arts.

Bolitho, Annie and Hutchinson, Mary. *Out of the Ordinary: Inventive ways of bringing communities, their stories and audiences to light.* Canberra Stories Group, Littlewood, Murrumbateman, New South Wales.
The authors have set out to re-frame, for a broad audience, the idea of what 'counts' as writing.

Cameron, Neil. *The Running and Stamping Book.* Illustrated by Faridah Whyte. Currency Press, 1995.
A series of warm-up exercises for groups. The author has drawn inspiration from a wide range of influences.

Clegg, Brian. *Instant Interviewing: Choose the right candidate now!* London: Kogan Page Ltd, 2001.
A small (112-page) and useful book that includes checklists related to the interviewing ask environment and interviewee information, as well as a range of questions interviewers ask in order to elicit the answers through which they improve their chances of selecting the best candidate for the job.

Community Arts Network, South Australia, 1999. A series of hint sheets:
Number 1: *A Seven Step Approach to Project Concept Development*
Number 2: *How to Look for Funding and Project Resources*
Number 3: *Legal and Industrial Issues in Project Management*
Number 4: *Preparing Funding Applications*

Coult, Tony and Kershaw, Baz. *Engineers of the Imagination*. Amazon, 1983.
> A guide to the basic techniques of Welfare State International, which, since 1968, has been developing a unique form of celebratory theatre.

Hawkes, Jon, for the Cultural Development Network (Victoria). *The Fourth Pillar of Sustainability: Culture's essential role in public planning*. Common Ground Publishing Pty Ltd, 2001.
> A discussion about how public planning should include an integrated framework for cultural evaluation.

Mead, Jemma. *Dancing Communities*. Sponsored by Arthritis Victoria with funds from Vic Health, 1999.
> A community workers' guide to conducting dance programs in community environments. An initiative of the Ausdance Active for Life Young Women's Dance Project.

National Forum of Community Dance Practitioners. *Moving On 2000*. The Australian Dance Council: Ausdance, New South Wales, 2000.
> Critical debate that emerged from the 2000 national forum for dance practitioners.

Philanthropy Australia Inc. *The Australian Directory of Philanthropy 2000–2001*, Melbourne, 2000. Published annually.
> A comprehensive reference of sources of non-government funding in Australia. Available through the organisation's bookshop: Level 10, 530 Collins Street, Melbourne 3000.

Poynor, Helen and Simmonds, Jacqueline (editors). *Dancers and Communities*. Australian Dance Council: Ausdance, New South Wales, 1997.
> A collection of writing about dance as a community art.

Williams, Denise. *From Idea to Application: A Practical Guide to Arts Project Development*. Community Arts Network, South Australia, 1996.
> Useful directions in development of an art project.

Women's Circus. *Women's Circus: Leaping Off the Edge*. Spinifex Press Ltd, 1997.
> A record of the history of the Women's Circus from 1991 to 1997.

## Online resources

CARC – Community Arts Resource Collection.
> A national collection of information about community arts, community cultural development, cultural policy and related topics.
> <www.vca.unimelb.edu.au/library/carc/index.html>

ORCA – Online Resource for Community-based Australian Arts.
> A 'culture and community activism' Web site. Includes articles, a project register, a project archive and a discussion bulletin board.
> <www.orca.on.net>

Australia's Cultural Network.
> An online gateway to Australia's cultural organisations, resources, activities and events.
> <www.acn.net.au>

Dramatic Online.
    'The Cultural Industry's Online Home':
    news and jobs to do with arts and culture.
    <www.dramaticonline.com>

Enter Artsmedia.
    Trainee recruitment and group training for
    the arts industry.
    <www.artsmedia.com.au>

Australian Business Arts Foundation.
    The site's aims are to increase private-sector
    support for arts and culture and to
    encourage people to reflect on what it is to
    be Australian.
    <www.abaf.org.au/abaf.html>

Philanthropy Australia.
    The national membership association that
    represents Australia's private, family and
    corporate trusts and foundations. Publishes
    the *Australian Directory of Philanthropy*.
    <www.philanthropy.org.au>

fuel4arts.
    A site of arts-marketing tools and ideas to
    take your work further, including resources,
    online forums and a newsletter.

GrantsLINK.
    The federal government's community-
    grants site.

Arts Law Centre of Australia.
    The site for the national community legal
    centre. Includes advice and information for
    artists and arts organisations about a wide
    range of issues, such as contracts, insurance
    and taxation. A good source for legal
    *pro formas* such as model contracts and
    release forms.
    <http://www.artslaw.asn.au/~artslaw>

Australian Copyright Council.
    The council provides advice about all
    copyright-related matters, and issues a range
    of useful information sheets and other
    publications.
    <http://www.copyright.org.au>

# Women's Circus: Leaping off the Edge

Adrienne Liebmann, Jen Jordan, Deb Lewis,
Louise Radcliffe-Brown, Patricia Sykes
and Jean Taylor (Eds.)


Established in 1991 as a community theatre project to work
with survivors of sexual assault, the Women's Circus toured
Beijing in 1995. Jugglers, acrobats, tricksters, aerialists,
technicians, administrators, musicians, designers and trainers tell
their story. *Women's Circus: Leaping off the Edge* tells the story of
the first five years of this extraordinary community project.


*This is a big, rowdy, colorful, three-ring circus of a book,
packed with death-defying feats and acts that will thrill and
amaze — not the least of which is their breathtaking
commitment to feminist process.*
**Carolyn Gage**


SBN: 1-875559-55-8

# If Passion Were a Flower ...
Lariane Fonseca

Inspired by the writing of Virginia Woolf and the painting of
Georgia O'Keefe, Lariane Fonseca uses the camera as a medium
through which to depict the passion of flowers.

ISBN: 1-875559-06-x

---

# Don't Shoot Darling:
# Women's Independent Film
# Making in Australia
Edited by Annette Blonski, Barbara Creed
and Freda Freiberg

*Don't Shoot Darling* is an important and fascinating record of
independent women's films in Australia.

ISBN: 0-86436-058-4

# Australia for Women: Travel and Culture

Edited by Susan Hawthorne and Renate Klein

An indispensable book for any woman travelling in Australia. It surveys the history of women in Australia as well as their contribution to the arts. It includes literature, film, the visual arts, music, circus and dance, as well as places of special significance to women, or simply beautiful places to be.

ISBN: 1-875559-27-2

---

# The Internet for Women

Rye Senjen and Jane Guthrey

*The Internet for Women* takes you on a magic-carpet ride to women-run sites around the world. It describes women's role in developing computers and in the development of on-line communities. A book which guides you through all the basic information you need to get started.

ISBN: 1-875559-52-3

If you would like to know more about Spinifex Press
write for a free catalogue or visit our website.

**$SPINIFEX PRESS**

PO Box 212 North Melbourne
Victoria 3051 Australia

**WITHDRAWN**